Brian Fleming Research & Learning Library
Ministry of Education
Ministry of Training, Colleges & Universities
900 Bay St. 13th Floor, Mowat Block
Toronto, ON M7A 1L2

EDUCATION IN A COMPETITIVE AND GLOBALIZING WORLD

EVIDENCE-BASED EDUCATION

EDUCATION IN A COMPETITIVE AND GLOBALIZING WORLD

Additional books in this series can be found on Nova's website under the Series tab.

Additional E-books in this series can be found on Nova's website under the e-books tab.

EDUCATION IN A COMPETITIVE AND GLOBALIZING WORLD

EVIDENCE-BASED EDUCATION

DENNIS FUNG CHUN-LOK
AND
VALERIE YIP WANG-YAN
EDITORS

Nova Science Publishers, Inc.
New York

Copyright © 2012 by Nova Science Publishers, Inc.

All rights reserved. No part of this book may be reproduced, stored in a retrieval system or transmitted in any form or by any means: electronic, electrostatic, magnetic, tape, mechanical photocopying, recording or otherwise without the written permission of the Publisher.

For permission to use material from this book please contact us:
Telephone 631-231-7269; Fax 631-231-8175
Web Site: http://www.novapublishers.com

NOTICE TO THE READER

The Publisher has taken reasonable care in the preparation of this book, but makes no expressed or implied warranty of any kind and assumes no responsibility for any errors or omissions. No liability is assumed for incidental or consequential damages in connection with or arising out of information contained in this book. The Publisher shall not be liable for any special, consequential, or exemplary damages resulting, in whole or in part, from the readers' use of, or reliance upon, this material. Any parts of this book based on government reports are so indicated and copyright is claimed for those parts to the extent applicable to compilations of such works.

Independent verification should be sought for any data, advice or recommendations contained in this book. In addition, no responsibility is assumed by the publisher for any injury and/or damage to persons or property arising from any methods, products, instructions, ideas or otherwise contained in this publication.

This publication is designed to provide accurate and authoritative information with regard to the subject matter covered herein. It is sold with the clear understanding that the Publisher is not engaged in rendering legal or any other professional services. If legal or any other expert assistance is required, the services of a competent person should be sought. FROM A DECLARATION OF PARTICIPANTS JOINTLY ADOPTED BY A COMMITTEE OF THE AMERICAN BAR ASSOCIATION AND A COMMITTEE OF PUBLISHERS.

Additional color graphics may be available in the e-book version of this book.

LIBRARY OF CONGRESS CATALOGING-IN-PUBLICATION DATA

Evidence-based education / editors, Dennis Fung Chun-Lok and Valerie Yip Wang-Yan.
  p. cm.
Includes index.
ISBN 978-1-61324-927-7 (hardcover)
 1. Effective teaching--Cross-cultural studies. 2. Teacher effectiveness--Cross-cultural studies. 3. Teaching--Evaluation--Cross-cultural studies. 4. Educational equalization--Cross-cultural studies. I. Fung, Dennis Chun-Lok. II. Yip, Valerie Wang-Yan.
 LB1025.3.E94 2011
 379.2'6--dc23
                                       2011018602

Published by Nova Science Publishers, Inc. † New York

CONTENTS

Preface vii

Chapter 1 In Search of Effective Pedagogies for Teaching Nature of Science: Perspective from an Experienced Teacher 1
Ching Lai and Benny Hin Wai Yung

Chapter 2 An Outdoor Educational Experience that Facilitates the Elevation of Self-Esteem but not the Negative Outcomes Often Associated with High Self-Esteem 21
Sarah Kafka, John A. Hunter, Mike Boyes, Jill Hayhurst, M. Stringer and Kerry O'Brien

Chapter 3 Critical Analysis of the Policies of School-Based Management in Hong Kong 57
Dennis Chun-Lok Fung and Valerie Wing-Yan Yip

Chapter 4 Parental Involvement in Children's Reading: A Cultural Perspective 71
Valerie W. Y. Yip and Dennis C. L. Fung

Chapter 5 Rural Elementary School Science Teacher Attitudes towards Varying Professional Development Strategies 95
Leonard A. Annetta, James Minogue, Michelle Cook, James A. Shymansky and Brandi Turmond

Chapter 6	An Investigation of Korean Gifted Education Teachers' Views on Leadership *Seung Hee Oh*	**111**
Index		**131**

PREFACE

This book presents significant results from around the globe in selected areas of research related to evidence-based education, especially in Hong Kong (SAR), New Zealand, China, Korea and America. Specifically, recent enthusiasm for 'evidence-based' practice in education has brought a new sense of development in the aspects of teaching and learning in primary and secondary schooling. This volume attempts to shed light on the proceedings of this development regarding hierarchical school system, school-based management, effective pedagogies, outdoor educational experience and teacher attitudes in these different areas.

Chapter 1 - Understanding nature of science (NOS) has long been regarded as a major component of scientific literacy and an important learning objective of science curricula in many countries. However teachers are, in general, lack of the knowledge and pedagogical skills necessary for teaching of NOS. This chapter reports a case study in Hong Kong on how teachers are prepared for this reform-oriented teaching. It concludes with a highlight of features of teacher professional development programs that are conducive for preparing teachers for the reform-oriented teaching.

Chapter 2 - Outdoor educational experiences have been shown to provide participants with heightened self-esteem. A growing body of evidence suggests, however, that high self-esteem also facilitates a variety of negative outcome behaviours with respect to self and others (i.e., drug and alcohol abuse, increased aggression and prejudice). In this study, the authors sought to determine whether undertaking a 10-day youth development voyage raised adolescents' self-esteem and negative outcome behaviours. Intervention and non-intervention participants completed measures of self-esteem at 4 separate times. Time 1 was 3 to 4 weeks before the voyage (T1). Time 2 was on the first day of the voyage (T2). Time 3 was on the last day of the voyage (T3). Time 4 was 4-5 months after the voyage (T4). Intervention participants also responded to scales assessing risky attitudes (i.e., towards drug and alcohol use), physical and verbal aggression, and racial and gender bias at each of the four time points. Participation in the voyage programme lead to increased self-esteem. No such effects were found for the non-intervention condition. Elevated self-esteem was maintained 4 to 5 months after voyage completion. Elevated self-esteem was not associated with corresponding increases in risky attitudes, aggression, or racial and gender bias. These findings suggest that participation in the developmental voyage produces elevated self-esteem that is both relatively enduring and free of negative outcomes.

Chapter 3 - Since the establishment of School-based Management (SBM) in Hong Kong in the 1990s, there have been substantial studies indicating that SBM has few, if any, significant benefits for secondary school students. This contradicts the SBM consultation paper, which stated that 'there is evidence of powerful links between the capacities that schools acquire with school-based management and learning outcomes for students though this was less the case in the 1980s and early 1990s, when school-based management tended to be a stand-alone initiative.'

Chapter 4 - This study aimed to understand how socially deprived parents in a Chinese society supported their children's reading at home. By examining the interview data gathered from questionnaires and interviews completed by the parents of second grade students, they were found to be supportive to reading with their children and to preparing a suitable environment for learning to read. Although the caregivers had a restricted understanding of their roles and of parent-child reading techniques, they nonetheless believed in their own capabilities. If they encountered difficulties, the families also tried to make use of their local networks. The parents transformed these beliefs into action in response to their role awareness and expectations of their children's future. Such beliefs and behaviours were strongly associated with their commitment to Chinese culture.

Chapter 5 - As part of a federally funded research initiative, elementary level science teachers' views regarding perceived effectiveness of four different professional development activities were investigated. Participants (n=259) from rural schools in the Midwestern United States participated in one of four different professional development (PD) activities: workshop, focus group, peer mentoring, and Interactive Television. Following participation in one of the four PD activities, participants were asked to provide feedback about the PD activity by completing a 5-point Likert scale survey consisting of

9 items, to help better understand teacher attitudes towards the various PD strategies and the overall effectiveness of the PD in promoting teacher pedagogical content knowledge (PCK). Study results indicated significant differences among teachers participating in the different PD activities in all of the nine post experience attitudinal-criteria.

Chapter 6 - Leadership skills have often been closely related to giftedness in giftedness research. The relationship between the concept of leadership and giftedness was made evident in the 'Marland Report.'

In: Evidence-Based Education ISBN: 978-1-61324-927-7
Editors: D. Chun-Lok and V. Wang-Yan © 2012 Nova Science Publishers, Inc.

Chapter 1

IN SEARCH OF EFFECTIVE PEDAGOGIES FOR TEACHING NATURE OF SCIENCE: PERSPECTIVE FROM AN EXPERIENCED TEACHER

Ching Lai[*] and Benny Hin Wai Yung
The University of Hong Kong, Hong Kong

ABSTRACT

Understanding nature of science (NOS) has long been regarded as a major component of scientific literacy and an important learning objective of science curricula in many countries.

However teachers are, in general, lack of the knowledge and pedagogical skills necessary for teaching of NOS. This chapter reports a case study in Hong Kong on how teachers are prepared for this reform-oriented teaching.

It concludes with a highlight of features of teacher professional development programs that are conducive for preparing teachers for the reform-oriented teaching.

Keywords: Nature of Science, Teacher Professional Development

---

[*]E-mail: lightchain@gmail.com

INTRODUCTION

Understanding nature of science (NOS) has long been regarded as a major component of scientific literacy and an important learning objective of science curricula in many countries (American Association for the Advancement of Science [AAAS], 1989, 1993; Council of Ministers of Education, Canada [CMEC], 1997; National Research Council [NRC], 1996). In line with this international trend, recent development of science curricula in Hong Kong has seen a shift from the predominantly content-focused goal to a wider goal of promoting understanding of nature of science (NOS). This poses a host of problems and challenges in preparing teachers for this new curriculum reform. For example, various studies consistently point to teachers' inadequate understanding of NOS (Lederman, 1992). Other studies also pointed out that, even teachers with sufficient NOS understanding, it is not automatically and necessarily translated into classroom practice (Lederman, 2007). Teachers are, in general, lack of the relevant pedagogical skills for the teaching of NOS. In view of this, a two-year teacher professional development (TPD) program was set up to prepare teachers in Hong Kong for the teaching of NOS. This chapter aims: firstly, to delineate the rationale underlying the design of the TPD program; secondly, to present a case of teacher learning to teach NOS and how various factors in the program had contributed to her learning.

THEORETICAL UNDERPINNINGS

This section first reviews early studies which attempted to improve teachers' understanding of NOS. It then analyzes three teacher professional development initiatives in details to delineate the rationale underlying the design of the TPD program which constitutes the context for the present study.

Searching for an Effective Approach of Teaching NOS

Much research efforts have been placed to improve teachers' conceptions of NOS for approximately fifty years. Some initial TPD programs which attempted to improve teachers' NOS understanding include the work of Welch and Walberg (1968). They investigated the usefulness of a summer institute program for physics teachers. Lavach (1969) discussed the historical development of some science concepts in an in-service program; and Billeh and Hasan (1975) conducted a four-week courses which included 12 lectures related to NOS. Lederman (1992), in his review, summarized that these efforts to improve teachers' understanding have met with some success, in a sense, that they have discussed historical aspects of development of scientific knowledge or drawn direct attention to the NOS.

Later on, Abd-El-Khalick and Lederman (2000) conducted another comprehensive review. The aim was to compare the 'effectiveness' of two different approaches to improve teachers' NOS conceptions: implicit and explicit approach. Implicit, as its name implied, assumes that learners would necessarily develop understanding of NOS as a result of engaging in science-related activities such as undertaking scientific inquiries. Whereas, explicit approach intentionally draws learners' attention to relevant aspects of NOS through instruction, discussion, questioning and written work following classroom activities that are geared towards various aspects of NOS. Based on the studies reviewed, Abd-El-Khalick and Lederman concluded that the explicit approach is relatively more effective in promoting teachers' NOS conceptions than the implicit one. Indeed, other evidence is accumulating to support this claim that an explicit approach, especially with a reflective component, is an effective way to improve teachers' understanding of NOS (e.g. Abd-El-Khalick, 2001; Abd-El-Khalick and Akerson, 2004; Bell, Lederman and Abd-El-Khalick, 2000; Irwin, 2000).

Teacher Professional Development Programs for Improving NOS Instruction

Improving teachers' understanding of NOS is a necessary, but not sufficient, condition for preparing them to teach NOS effectively to their students. In view of this, there has been a new wave of research efforts and TPD programs taking on the challenge of preparing teachers for effective NOS instruction in a more holistic manner. In addition to sharpening teachers' NOS understanding, this entails developing their pedagogical content knowledge (PCK) (Shulman 1986, 1987) for teaching of NOS as well as the necessary teaching skills and techniques. Because of limited space, only three studies are reviewed.

The first study was carried out by Akerson and Hanuscin (2007) in the context of a three-year TPD program aiming at preparing elementary teachers for NOS teaching. The study traced the participants' views of NOS, the instructional practice they used to facilitate students to establish appropriate NOS views, and the influence of participants' instruction on elementary students' NOS views. The design of the TPD program mainly drew on Bell and Gilbert's (1996) science teacher development model. The model emphasizes three components: (a) personal development, in which the teacher must be aware that there is a need for professional development and acknowledges the desire to acquire new ideas or strategies; (b) social development, in which the teachers have opportunities to discuss ideas with other teachers, and to collectively renegotiate what it means to teach science and be a teacher of science; and (c) professional development, in which the teachers are supported in implementing the new ideas and strategies in their classroom practice, drawing on the changes they make personally and socially. These three components are viewed as essential to build on teachers' commitment to enact changes in their own classrooms and professional communities. Other features of successful teacher development models that were also found in Akerson and Hanuscin's TPD program included: providing enough time to allow for acquisition of new views along with practice, feedback and follow-up; allowing the teacher to reflect on the new ideas or implementation of the new skills; and allowing the teacher to see the new skills or strategies in practice (Henriques, 1998; Loucks-Horsley, Hewson, Love, and Stiles, 2003). The TPD program finally developed a series of monthly half-day workshops, as well as regular on-site classroom visits by project staff. Results indicated that the teachers (as well as the students they taught) showed positive changes in their views of NOS and improved science pedagogy. According to the authors, all aspects of the program had influenced teachers positively to varied degrees. In particular, the individual support for teachers was considered to be a critical element contributing to their social development such as meeting and discussing with like-minded colleagues. Participating teachers also reflected that the monthly workshops had had an impact on their NOS understanding, as well as their instructional practice.

The positive outcomes outlined above informed the design of our TPD program. Due attention were paid to the three components of Bell and Gilbert's TPD model. First, teachers participating in the present study were those who felt insecure about NOS teaching but committed to improve their science teaching (as they all joined our program on a voluntary basis). This, according to Bell and Gilbert's (1996) assertion, and supported by Akerson et al.'s (2007) study, is an important, first step in the teachers' personal development. Corresponding to the second component in Bell et al.'s model, i.e. social development, teachers in our program were offered ample opportunities to engage in discourse with peers regarding their practice in meetings and workshops. Regarding the third component (i.e. professional development), teachers were offered individual support from experienced facilitators during the trial out of newly learnt ideas and strategies in their own classroom.

The second study which has informed the design of our TPD program is Project ICAN (Inquiry, Context, and Nature of Science). It was a five-year TPD project funded by the National Science Foundation in the United States (Kim, Ko, Lederman and Lederman, 2005). Of interest and relevant to the present study is its requirement of the participants to undertake some microteaching sessions in order to improve their pedagogical skills related to NOS teaching. In Project ICAN, microteaching refers to a peer teaching presentation that mimics what teachers plan to do with their students. These lessons were collaboratively planned and delivered by teams of teachers. A teacher team consisted of three to four members who were voluntarily changed for each peer teaching assignment. Each lesson was videotaped and afterwards, there was a brief discussion of the aspects of NOS addressed, as well as ways the lesson could be further improved.

Results indicate that, over the five years of the ICAN Project, peer microteaching experiences appeared to be an important professional development experience. These opportunities allowed teachers to become more familiar with teaching NOS and helped them reflect and develop their PCK on NOS teaching. In addition, the development of teachers' pedagogical skills related to NOS teaching in Years 4 and 5 of the project was found to be consistent with students' improved understanding of NOS as revealed by analyses of student work. Based on this finding, Lederman and his colleagues (Lederman, Lederman, Kim, and Ko,.2006) argued that TPD programs should provide teachers with opportunities to plan and implement explicit NOS instruction, and to observe and discuss peers' microteaching lessons.

While acknowledging the value of creating opportunities for teachers to learn from their peers, we argue that professional learning can be more profound and effective if videotapes of NOS instruction in authentic classroom situations are shared among the participants. This is because microteaching in front of peers cannot reflect the real classroom situations. To overcome this limitation, teachers participated in our program were asked to share and examine videotapes of themselves teaching NOS in authentic classroom situations.

Of significant import on the design of our TPD program was a study by Bartholomew, Osborne and Ratcliffe (2004). It reports the work undertaken with a group of 11 teachers in a year to teach different aspects of nature of science including the processes and practices undertaken by scientists in generation of scientific knowledge. Their TPD program consisted of development of curriculum materials, classroom trial-run teaching and follow-up workshops. In this project, teachers were asked to develop curriculum materials in the beginning stage of the study. During the first three months of the study, four initial one-day meetings were held. These meetings provided participating teachers an opportunity to explore, plan, and develop materials for the explicit teaching of NOS. However, that had turned out to be a difficult task for teachers to design curriculum materials which explicitly address NOS elements. The researchers therefore drew from a range of existing sources (e.g. Goldsworthy, Watson, and Wood-Robinson, 2000; Ratcliffe, 1999) and worked out lesson outlines and some instructional materials. The researchers later modeled their conception of good practice for the effective teaching of NOS with the developed materials. Such models were offered as framework that teachers could try and adapt. The teachers then worked in groups (according to the grade level they taught) to share, develop and adapt the modeled materials and approaches with their own ideas. Teachers then tried out the adapted materials and undertook lessons over a period of two terms.

Drawing on the data collected through field notes, videos of the teachers' lessons, teachers' reflective diaries, and instruments that measured their understanding of NOS and their views on the purposes and worthiness of carrying out discussion in the classroom, Bartholomew et al. (2004) explored the factors that afforded or inhibited the teachers' pedagogic performance in teaching of NOS. They organized these factors into a framework they referred to as *The Five Dimensions of Practice.* In brief, they argued that effective teaching of NOS requires establishing a context in which it is possible for students to engage in reflexive epistemic dialogue. It requires teachers to shift their conception of their role from the dispenser of knowledge to a facilitator of learning; a change in their classroom discourse to one which is more open and dialogic; a shift in their conception of the learning goals of science lessons from merely gain in subject knowledge to one which incorporates the development of reasoning and an understanding of the epistemic basis of belief in science; and the development of classroom activities which are owned by students and relevant to their daily life. The five dimensions of effective NOS instruction suggested above provided an initial framework for guiding the design of activities for our TPD program. It had had also an important bearing on the design of the data collection instruments as well as the analysis of data at subsequent stages of the present study.

METHOD AND CONTEXT OF THE STUDY

This interpretive study on teacher learning was situated in a two-year TPD program preparing teachers for teaching NOS. Below is a brief recap to highlight the three distinct features of the program. This is followed by a description of the data sources and methods used to analyse and report the learning of an experienced teacher in her course of participation in the TPD program.

Feature 1: Provision of Curriculum Resources

The decision to provide teachers with curriculum materials for their trial lessons was informed by Bartholomew et al.'s study (2004) where they found teachers experiencing difficulties in designing their own curriculum materials. In this study, 17 sets of curriculum materials were developed for NOS teaching across the biology curriculum using an explicit and reflective approach. The design of the materials was guided by the notion of *educative* curriculum materials (Ball and Cohen, 1996; Davis and Krajcik, 2005). Teachers were invited to choose two sets of curriculum materials, to modify and adapt to their own situations before they used them in their own classes.

Feature 2: Use of Authentic Classroom Videos

Other than being informed by the three studies discussed, the decision to use video to facilitate teacher professional development is also supported by a body of literature. In her review of research in this area, Sherin (2004), identifies several affordances that videos can provide for teacher professional development - video as a lasting record; video can be collected and edited; and video provides opportunities for teachers to acquire a new "analytic mind set" to look at classroom teaching (p.13). In short, through watching and analyzing classroom videos, teachers have the opportunity to develop a different kind of knowledge for teaching – knowledge not of 'what to do next', but knowledge of how to *interpret* and *reflect* on classroom practices. It is this kind of knowledge that our TPD program aimed to develop in teachers. In connection to this, Bartholomew et al.'s (2004) *Five Dimension of Practice* was introduced to teachers as a framework guiding their interpretation and reflection on the videos. Such guidance, in the form of providing an analytic framework, is vital to teachers to make sense of the teaching practice shown in the videos, and thereby develop the ability to 'notice' and interpret what is happening in their own and others' classrooms. This echoes the call by van Es and Sherin (2008) for advancing the notion of 'learning to notice' while teachers are engaging in video-mediated professional development activities. Lastly, our use of authentic classroom videos was also informed by the literature on preparing teachers for reform-oriented teaching (e.g. Black and Atkin, 1996; Putnam and Borko, 2000) which highlights the limited opportunities for teachers to experience workable alternatives to conventional practice in actual classroom settings. In brief, our TPD program makes use of videos showing teachers teaching NOS in authentic classroom situations as the main tool to mediate teachers' learning of how to teach NOS. Specifically, the trial lessons of teachers teaching NOS were videotaped. Selected video clips were then shared, analyzed and discussed among the teachers in study group meetings and workshops with reference to the framework of *Five Dimension of Practice*.

Feature 3: Organization of Study Groups

It appears that in all the three TPD programs reviewed, peer learning did play a role in helping teachers learning how to teach NOS. In our program, the teachers were provided with opportunities not only to learn from peers in the form of study groups, but to decide on their own agenda for their professional development in learning how to teach NOS. For example, they were asked to select video episodes which they wanted to bring up for discussion in addition to those selected by the facilitators. Such collaboration not only established connection between teachers' classroom experience and the video used, it also delivered a message that the professional developers respected and welcomed teachers' contribution. We reckoned that this can be important in establishing communication norms and building trust in a learning community.

An overview of the TPD Program

About 20 secondary biology teachers formed themselves into three study groups, each with about six to seven teachers and facilitated by a science educator. The teachers worked collaboratively in study group meetings to help each other to learn how to teach NOS. To start with, the teachers were given curriculum materials for teaching NOS using an explicit and reflective approach. They refined the resources and taught the modified curriculum materials in their own classrooms. The lesson videos were then shared and analyzed collaboratively in the study group meetings. Towards the end of the two-year program, the three study groups came together to share their experiences on themes of common interests in their process of learning how to teach NOS. The major TPD activities were listed in Table 1.

Table 1. Major activities in the TPD program

Major TPD activities	Descriptions
Briefing session	• Introduce the objectives and the professional support provided by the TPD program
Planning meeting	• Form teachers into study groups; who then work out their own learning agenda • Introduce strategies for teaching NOS • Initiate teachers to begin with the process of refining the curriculum resources to cater for their own settings'
Two-day training workshops on teaching NOS	• Consolidate teachers' knowledge base on NOS and the relevant pedagogical content knowledge (PCK) for the teaching of NOS • Discussion topics include: common myths about NOS; planning a lesson on NOS; teaching NOS across a series of lessons; consolidating NOS learning; teaching NOS on unplanned occasions
Pre-trial run discussion	• discuss the lesson plan and the refined teaching materials with the facilitator
Trial lesson	• Teach the NOS lesson via an explicit and reflective approach using the refined curriculum materials
Post-lesson discussion	• Reflect on and discuss the trial lesson with the facilitator
Study group meetings	• Review and analyze trial lesson videos to look for ways of improvement
Thematic workshops	• Discuss and share exemplary video cases contributed by each of the study groups
Debriefing meeting	• Teachers share and celebrate with their peers on their experience in learning to teach NOS

Research Methodology and Data Sources

This study is a naturalistic study of a teacher's experience to search for effective pedagogies for teaching of NOS. For triangulation purposes, multiple data sources were employed in constructing the case of teacher learning reported below. These include: (1) the reflection tasks completed by the teacher after her two NOS lessons and the corresponding follow-up interviews; (2) the reflection tasks completed by the teacher after reviewing the two NOS lesson videos and the corresponding follow-up interviews; (3) e-mail correspondents, telephone conversations and face-to-face discussions with the TPD facilitator concerning planning and teaching of the two NOS lessons; and the researcher's lesson observation and field notes.

Interpretations of the data collected were constructed using a method similar to that described by Erickson (1986, p.119), focusing on the 'immediate and local meanings of actions', as defined by the case teacher. Accordingly, the prime aim was to find out, from the perspective of the teacher what was happening in her classroom and why she acted in certain ways. This was done by analyzing the lesson videos in relation to the data collected and linking them to what the teacher saw as significant in her course of learning to teach NOS.

Narrative accounts will be used to convey the context of this study and the experiences that were implicit in the story of learning to teach NOS of the case teacher, and of ourselves as participant observers in various TPD events. In this way, we feel that we could emphasize the voice of the teacher in a credible manner, and emphasise our interpretations in the latter part of the chapter. Pseudonym is used for the teacher in the accounts below.

NARRATIVE ACCOUNTS

Maria is an experienced teacher who has taught biology for more than 20 years. She is very enthusiastic in professionally upgrading herself. This was the second time for her to join a similar TPD program on preparing teachers for NOS teaching. This time, one of the key learning Maria mentioned in her reflection tasks was the importance of providing adequate time for student discussion. In the narrative accounts below, the journey of how Maria attained her important learning of "not to hurry things" in teaching NOS, as well as how various factors in the TPD programs had contributed to her learning will be discussed.

Learning from the First NOS Lesson on Discovery of the Cause of Gastric Ulcer

1) Planning the Lesson

One week prior to her teaching, Maria sent the lesson plan and refined teaching materials to the TPD facilitator for comment and advice. In line with the *Five Dimensions of Effective Practice*'s call for the teacher being a facilitator of learning, more authentic activities, as well as open and dialogic classroom discourses, Maria incorporated four rounds of discussion in her original lesson plan, followed by students' poster presentations, a whole class discussion, lecturing and a video review on a 10 minutes' clip showing a TV interview with Dr. Barry Marshall, the scientist of the discovery.

During the pre-lesson discussions, the TPD facilitator commended Maria for her efforts in designing teaching-learning activities that are in line of what the program advocates. However, in view of the limited lesson time available (90 minutes), Maria was advised to trim some contents so as to leave ample time for the group discussions. Even though Maria had agreed to trim down part of the contents, she still failed to leave adequate time for the student discussions during the lesson.

2) Reflecting on the Lesson

When asked about what she had learned from teaching the lesson and the difficulties she had encountered, the first sentence Maria wrote in her reflection task was:

'I should have left more time for class interaction and group discussion.'

She recalled in one of the group discussions (on the proposal of hypothesis), students had had disagreement among themselves, but she had not given them enough time for their discussion:

'… if I have enough time, I would ask students to clarify what they think, or to give comments to each others' ideas…I realize that when I was planning the lesson, I did not think exhaustively enough. After the lesson, I understand that it would be better if there was a bit more time for discussion.'

In a follow-up interview, Maria explained how she had come to be aware of the problem. She pinpointed that the peer interaction with other teachers during the study group meeting had helped her to reflect on this learning.

"I have been teaching for so many years…and may not be sensitive enough to aware of my own weaknesses in teaching. If somebody observe my lesson (other teachers and the TPD facilitator), they can remind me and tell me which part I can improve. Their opinions are more objective."

3) Reviewing the Classroom Video

In response to a question on the accompanying task sheet, 'Write down the new insights gained from reflecting on the lesson's video, Maria put down:

'Wait time is very important, do not hurry students.'

In the follow-up interview, Maria explained how she had benefited from reviewing and reflecting on her own lesson video.

'After I have watched the video, I try to remind myself one thing. Whenever I teach NOS, which requires high-order thinking, I should give more time for the students to think deeply. I do not want them to feel that they have to rush. Even if I say "You don't have to hurry", I am actually pushing them…Because I saw from my video that I did say "We have to be faster" during the lesson…'

Learning from the Second NOS Lesson on the Discovery of the Function of Nucleus

1) Planning the Lesson

Two months later, Maria conducted another lesson with an explicit focus on NOS teaching. She did not follow the teaching plan suggested in the teaching package this time.

Instead, she chose to spend time on discussing questions in the pre-lesson task that came along with the teaching package. She planned to discuss 11 questions in a 90-minute lesson. Apparently, she wanted to make the lesson more open and dialogic. Again, the facilitator commented that there were too many questions and student might not have time to discuss all the questions thoroughly.

During a follow-up interview, Maria appreciated the advice and support she received from the facilitator during the planning stage. She said the pre-lesson discussion had helped her to iron out only a few of the key questions for students to discuss in the lesson. It also reminded her how to better allocate the time for student discussion.

"The facilitator did remind me to let students work on the questions individually first before asking them to discuss with their groupmates⋯ In the end, allotting three minutes for students to work on the questions individually was just too demanding for them. Therefore I learned how to better allocate the time; how to decide on which question to be discussed in the limited lesson time are important."

2) Reflecting on the Lesson

Similar to her experience in the first NOS lesson, time management continued to be a main concern for Maria as revealed in her reflection task of the second NOS lesson. Below are a few of the relevant excerpts:

'There were a lot of learning materials in my lesson plan so I needed to decide which part had to be cut.'

'It was difficult to allocate the appropriate amount of time for students to work on the questions individually, and then to participate in group discussion and presentation'

'Time control in group discussion is much more difficult than what I thought.'

In the reflection task, Maria also recalled how she did manage not to rush students to finish the discussion in this second trial NOS lesson.

'I did not allocate enough time for the discussion. I was a bit in hurry. The discussion was a bit overrun. But finally I managed to let it go. I told myself that just give them more time to discuss… do not rush the lesson…'

Overall speaking, Maria treasured the time she spent on discussing the questions with the students. In her reflection, she indicated that she would rather increase the time given for students' discussions for at least *4 times*. As she put it:

'I think the questions are worth discussing because students can have the opportunity to think, to discuss and to argue. If I were to conduct the lesson again, I would do it in three lessons instead of two.'

In response to the last question of the reflection task, 'Is there anything you would like to share about learning to teach NOS with others?' Maria put down *'wait time'*.

3) Reviewing the Classroom Video

In reviewing and reflecting on her lesson video, Maria highlighted several episodes where she was concerned about her time management for class discussion. For example:

> 'For the first group discussion on ... , I should have allowed ample time for group discussion.'

> '(It is) good to allow students to think on their own before getting into group discussion, especially for questions which are more demanding. The " Think Time" is important'.

Reflecting on the Learning Journey as a Whole

Reflecting on the journey of learning to teach NOS, Maria found that her personal belief about teaching, her experience of teaching these two NOS lessons, sharing with the peers and the facilitator, the opportunity for her to review her own classroom videos had contributed to her learning about the paramount importance of good time management in conducting discussions with students on NOS ideas.

DISCUSSION

An explicit and reflective approach of teaching NOS has been advocated as an effective way of teaching NOS for quite some time (e.g. Abd-El-Khalick and Akerson, 2004). In Maria's case, she planned her lesson using an explicit and reflective approach. She did provide students with a lot of opportunities to experience the kind of discussions that scientists normally undertake in scientific inquiry. However, insufficient time was allotted to the activities. This resulted in students not gaining sufficient experiences of which they could subsequently reflect on; and hence affecting the effectiveness of the lesson (as expressed by Maria). In other words, Maria had come to grips with the essence of what it means by a reflective approach, i.e., 'leaving enough time for student discussion' is a prerequisite for adopting a reflective approach in teaching NOS. Without enough time for discussion, students will not have adequate first-hand experiences to reflect. This, in turns, will affect their NOS understanding. Implied in Maria's understanding of the importance of allowing students with sufficient time *'to think, to discuss and to argue'* is a deep understanding of learning NOS concepts as a 'cognitive' rather than an affective learning outcome (Abd-El-Khalick and Lederman, 2000). This is also in agreement with what Bartholomew et al.'s (2004) call for a context in which it is possible for students to engage in reflexive epistemic dialogue. This change in pedagogical practices requires teachers to shift in the conception of their own role from the dispenser of knowledge to a facilitator of learning; a change in their classroom discourse to one which is more open and dialogic; a shift in their conception of the learning goals of science lessons from merely gain in subject knowledge to one which incorporates the development of reasoning and an understanding of the epistemic basis of belief in science; and the development of classroom activities which are owned by students and relevant to their daily life.

In fact, the importance of wait time for effective teaching in general has long been stressed in the research literature and is well encapsulated by Rowe's (1986) paper entitled *Wait time: Slowing down may be a way of speeding up!* In his review on math and science studies, Tobin (1987) also came to a conclusion that wait time appears to facilitate higher cognitive level learning by providing teachers and students with additional time to think. However, allow more time for student to discuss and have a long wait time is often 'easy said than done' (e.g. Jegede and Olajide, 1995). Maria is a case in point. This seemingly trivial and simple learning did not come easy but after a lot of inputs from the peers and TPD facilitator at different stages of the TPD program including pre- and post-lesson discussions, reviewing and reflecting on the lesson videos, sharing and discussion in study group meetings. Based on Maria's case, we argue that previous TPD efforts might have underestimated the difficulties and effort required to make teachers *realizing* 'the importance of leaving adequate time for student discussion and have long wait time' for teaching in general and teaching of NOS in particular. We suspect that much greater efforts will be needed to help teachers improve their practices in this area.

The above findings also provide glimpses of how features of the TPD program had contributed to Maria's learning. For example, the provision of NOS teaching materials provides an initial picture of how an explicit and reflective approach of teaching NOS is like. When Maria modified and adapted the curriculum materials, she was actually "learning" how an explicit and reflective approach of teaching NOS is like. In planning the lessons, she was guided by the analytic framework of *Five Dimensions of Practice*, Besides, as noted by Maria, the facilitator's on-site comments and peer's comments in study group meetings were important reminders to her teaching. Without these comments, Maria might not have notified where she could make further improvement. She might not realize "wait time" was an important learning to her, even though she is a teacher with 20 years of teaching experience.

Findings of the present study also provide empirical support to claims that learning is more meaningful when it is embedded in the practice (e.g. Lieberman, 1996). The provision of the trial practice served Maria with first-hand NOS teaching experience. As shown in the findings and her reflection, she learned most in teaching the two NOS lessons with the second trial experience echoing and reinforcing those attained in the first trial lesson.

Lastly, findings of this study also provide empirical support to the claim that video can afford fine-grain analyses of teaching (Sherin, 2004) and that, such analyses can be enhanced by providing teachers with an analytic framework such as the *Five Dimensions of Practice*. As evident in Maria's case, because of the opportunities for detailed analyses of her videos using the analytical framework provided, she was able to "see" from her video where she urged students to move faster in their discussions and she was also able to notice where she could do much better.

CONCLUSION

In sum, we argue that an effective TPD program for helping teachers to learn how to teach NOS should consider the provision of NOS teaching resources, opportunities for trial teaching in authentic classroom situations, discussion with peers and knowledgeable others, and above all, the opportunity to review and reflect on their own classroom videos guided by an appropriate theoretical framework.

REFERENCES

Abd-El-Khalick, F. (2001). Embedding nature of science instruction in preservice elementary science courses: Abandoning scientism, but.... *Journal of Research in Science Teaching, 12* (3), 215 – 233.

Abd-El-Khalick, F., and Akerson, V. L. (2004). Learning as conceptual change: Factors mediating the development of preservice elementary teachers' views of nature of science. *Science Education, 88*, 785 – 810.

Abd-El-Khalick, F., and Lederman, N. G. (2000). Improving science teachers' conceptions of nature of science: A critical review of the literature. *International Journal of Science Education, 22* (7), 665 – 701.

Akerson, V. L., and Hanuscin, D. L. (2007). Teaching Nature of Science through Inquiry: Results of a 3-Year Professional Development Program. *Journal of Research in Science Education, 44* (5), 653 – 680.

American Association for the Advancement of Science [AAAS]. (1989). *Project 2061: Science for all Americans.* New York: Oxford University Press.

American Association for the Advancement of Science [AAAS]. (1993). *Benchmarks for scientific literacy.* New York: Oxford University Press.

Ball, D. L., and Cohen, D. K. (1996). Reform by the book: What is –or might be –the role of curriculum materials in teacher learning and instructional reform? *Educational Researcher, 25* (9), 6 - 14.

Bartholomew, H., Osborne, J., and Ratcliffe, M. (2004). Teaching students "ideas-about-science": Five dimensions of effective practice. *Science Education, 88*, 655 – 682.

Bell, B., and Gilbert, J. (1996). *Teacher development: A model from science education.* London: Falmer Press.

Bell, R. L., Lederman, N. G., and Abd-El-Khalick, F. (2000). Developing and acting upon one's conception of the nature of science: A follow-up study. *Journal of Research in Science Teaching, 37* (6), 563 – 581.

Billeh, V., and Hasan, O. (1975). Factors affecting teachers' gain in understanding the nature of science. *Journal of Research in Science Teaching, 12*(3), 209-219.

Black, P., and Atkin, J. A. (1996). *Changing the subject: Innovations in science, mathematics and technology education.* London: Routledge.

Council of Ministers of Education, Canada [CMEC]. (1997). *Common Framework of Science Learning Outcomes.* Toronto, Canada: CMEC.

Davis, E. A., and Krajcik, J. S. (2005). Designing educative curriculum materials to promote teacher learning. *Educational Researcher, 34* (4), 3-14.

Goldsworthy, A., Watson, R., and Wood-Robinson, V. (2000). Developing understanding in scientific enquiry. Hatfield: Association for Science Education.

Henriques, L. (1998). *Maximizing the impact of your in-service: Designing the inservice and selecting the participants.* Paper presented at the annual meeting of the Association for the Education of Teachers of Science, Minneapolis, MN.

Irwin, A. (2000). Historical case studies: teaching the nature of science in context. *Science Education, 84,* 5 – 26.

Jegede, O. J., and Olajide, J. O. (1995). Wait-time, classroom discourse, and the influence of sociocultural factors in science teaching. *Science Education, 79* (3), 233-249.

Kim, B. S., Ko, E. K., Lederman, N. G., and Lederman, J. S. (2005, April). *A Developmental Continuum of Pedagogical Content Knowledge for Nature of Science Instruction.* Paper Presented at the Annual Meeting of the National Association for Research in Science Teaching, Dallas, Texas.

Lavach, J. F. (1969). Organization and evaluation of an in-service program in the history of science. *Journal of Research in Science Teaching, 6*(2), 166-170.

Lederman, N. G. (1992). Students' and teachers' conceptions of the nature of science: A review of the Research. *Journal of Research in Science Teaching, 29*(4), 331-359.

Lederman, N. G. (2007). Nature of science: past, present, and future. In S. K. Abell and N. G. Lederman (Eds.), *Handbook of research on science education* (pp. 831-880). London: Lawrence Erlbaum Associates.

Lederman, N. G., Lederman, J. S., Kim, B. S., and Ko, E. K. (2006). *Project ICAN: A Program to enhance teachers and students' understandings of nature of science and scientific inquiry.* Paper presented at the Annual Meeting of the National Association for Research in Science Teaching, San Francisco, CA.

Lieberman, A. (1996). Practices that support teacher development: transforming conceptions of professional learning. In M. W. McLaughlin and I. Oberman (Eds.), *Teacher Learning: New Policies, New Practices* (pp. 185-201). New York: Teachers College Press.

Loucks-Horsley, S., Hewson, P. W., Love, N. B., and Stiles, K. E. (2003). *Designing professional development for teachers of science and mathematics.* Thousand Oaks, CA: Corwin Press.

National Research Council [NRC]. (1996). *National science education standards.* Washington, DC: National Academic Press.

Putnam, R. T., and Borko, H. (1997). Teacher Learning: Implications of New Views of Cognition. In B. Biddle, T. L. Good and I. F. Goodson (Eds.), *International handbook of teachers and teaching, Vol. II* (pp.1223-1296). Dordrecht: Kluwer Academic Publishers.

Ratcliffe, M. (1999). Evaluation of abilities in interpreting media reports of scientific research. *International Journal of Science Education, 21*(10), 1085 – 1999.

Rowe, M.B. (1986). Wait time: Slowing down may be a way of speeding up! *Journal of Teacher Education, 37*(1), 43-50.

Sherin, M. G. (2004). New perspectives on the role of video in teacher education. In J. Brophy (Ed.), *Using video in teacher education* (pp. 1–27). Oxford, UK: Elsevier.

Shulman, L. S. (1986). Those who understand: knowledge growth in teaching. *Educational Researcher,* 15, 4-14.

Shulman, L. S. (1987). Knowledge and teaching: foundations of the new reform. *Harvard Educational Review,* 57, 1-22.

Tobin, K. (1987). The role of wait time in higher cognitive level learning. *Review of Educational Research, 57*(1), 69-95.

van Es, E.A. and Sherin, M.G. (2008). Mathematics Teachers' "Learning to Notice" in the Context of a Video Club. *Teaching and Teacher Education, 24*(2), 244–276.

Welch, W. W., and Walberg, H. J. (1968). An evaluation of summer institute programs for physics teachers. *Journal of Research in Science Teaching, 5*(2), 105- 109.

In: Evidence-Based Education
Editors: D. Chun-Lok and V. Wang-Yan © 2012 Nova Science Publishers, Inc.
ISBN: 978-1-61324-927-7

Chapter 2

AN OUTDOOR EDUCATIONAL EXPERIENCE THAT FACILITATES THE ELEVATION OF SELF-ESTEEM BUT NOT THE NEGATIVE OUTCOMES OFTEN ASSOCIATED WITH HIGH SELF-ESTEEM

Sarah Kafka, John A. Hunter, Mike Boyes, Jill Hayhurst, M. Stringer and Kerry O'Brien
Department of Psychology, University of Otago, New Zealand

Outdoor educational experiences have been shown to provide participants with heightened self-esteem. A growing body of evidence suggests, however, that high self-esteem also facilitates a variety of negative outcome behaviours with respect to self and others (i.e., drug and alcohol abuse, increased aggression and prejudice). In this study, we sought to determine whether undertaking a 10-day youth development voyage raised adolescents' self-esteem and negative outcome behaviours. Intervention and non-intervention participants completed measures of self-esteem at 4 separate times. Time 1 was 3 to 4 weeks before the voyage (T1). Time 2 was on the first day of the voyage (T2). Time 3 was on the last day of the voyage (T3). Time 4 was 4-5 months after the voyage (T4). Intervention participants also responded to scales assessing risky attitudes (i.e., towards drug and alcohol use), physical and verbal aggression, and racial and gender bias at each of the four time points. Participation in the voyage programme lead to increased self-esteem. No such effects were found for the non-intervention condition. Elevated self-esteem was maintained 4 to 5 months after voyage completion. Elevated self-esteem was not associated with corresponding increases in risky attitudes, aggression, or racial and gender bias. These findings suggest that participation in the developmental voyage produces elevated self-esteem that is both relatively enduring and free of negative outcomes.

A large body of research has revealed that undertaking outdoor interventions can increase participants' self-esteem (e.g., Kelly and Baer, 1969; Marsh and Richards, 1988, 1990; Marsh, Richards, and Barnes, 1986a,b; Norris and Weinman, 1996; see also Hattie, Marsh, Neill, and Richards, 1997) and that these increases endure after programme completion (e.g., Grocott, and Hunter, 2009; Marsh et al., 1986a). In recent years however, studies have begun to link the attainment of high self-esteem with a range of costs (for reviews see Baumeister, Campbell, Krueger, and Vohs, 2003; Emler. 2001), prompting some researchers to recommend that the pursuit of self-esteem be avoided (e.g., Crocker and Park, 2004). Yet other theorists have countered that it is the manner in which self-esteem is sought that determines whether high self-esteem is associated with negative outcomes and proposals regarding the way in which to pursue self-esteem without incurring costs have been put forth (e.g., DuBois and Flay, 2004; Pyszczynski and Cox, 2004; Sheldon, 2004). The purpose of this study is to examine whether undertaking a developmental sailing voyage enhances participants' self-esteem and whether these increases are maintained after the programme has ended. Further, this study will assess whether self-esteem increases occur without corresponding increases in costly attitudes and behaviour.

Research shows that there are an array of benefits associated with high self-esteem (e.g., Brown and McGill, 1989; Cozzarelli, 1993; Di Paula and Campbell, 2002; Dodgson and Wood, 1998; Galinsky and Ku, 2004; Hall, Kotch, Browne, and Rayens, 1996; Hobfoll and Leiberman, 1987; Murray et al., 2002; Pennix, van Tilburg, Boeke, Deeg, Kriegsman, and van Eijk, 1998; Rector and Roger, 1997; Robins, Tracy, Trzesniewski, Potter, and Gosling, 2001; Shimizu and Pelham, 2004; Wood, Heimpel, and Michela, 2003; Wood, Heimpel, Newby-Clark, and Ross, 2005; for reviews, see DuBois and Flay, 2004; Leary, 1999b). Evidence for the pitfalls linked with low self-esteem is similarly extensive (e.g., Crocker and Luhtanen, 2003; Murray, Rose, Bellavia, Holmes, and Kusche, 2002; Perez, Pettit, David, Kistner, and Joiner, 2001; Wood, Heimpel, and Michela, 2003; see Harter, 2003 for a review of findings). It is hardly surprising to note, therefore, that many studies have examined the utility of programmes aimed at enhancing self-esteem (e.g., Dijksterhuis, 2004; Hall and Tarrier, 2003; Joseph and Greenberg, 2001; Kiernan, Gormley, and Maclachlan, 2004; McGovern, Guida, and Corey, 2002; for a review, see Harter, 1998).

A growing body of research suggests that taking part in outdoor interventions may be successful in this regard (see Hattie, Marsh, Neill, and Richards, 1997). Thus, the findings from several studies have revealed increased self-esteem amongst those who take part in that such programmes (e.g., Kelly and Baer, 1969; Marsh and Richards, 1988, 1990; Marsh, Richards, and Barnes, 1986a,b). Research examining the capacity of sailing interventions to enhance participants' self-esteem is, however, lacking despite the fact that sailing programmes are in relatively widespread operation globally (Hunter, Boyes, Maunsell, and O'Hare, 2002). The few studies that have been carried out show that not only do participants (or trainees) experience self-esteem increases over the course of a sailing intervention (Grocott and Hunter, 2009; Norris and Weinman, 1996), but these improvements occur in as a little as 10 days and self-esteem increases are maintained three months after the voyage (Grocott and Hunter, 2009).

Research indicating that there are costs associated with high self-esteem (for reviews, see Baumeister et al., 2003; Emler. 2001) presents a threat to the rationale behind interventions aimed at improving people's self-esteem, however. High self-esteem has been linked with increased drug and alcohol use (see Karatzias et al., 2001; Scheier, Botvin, Griffin, and Diaz, 2000; for a review, see Baumeister et al., 2003; Emler. 2001), amplified physical and verbal aggression (see Baumeister et al., 1996; Salmivalli, Kaukiainen, Kaistaniemi, and Lagerspetz, 1999; van Boxtel, Orobio de Castro, and Goossens, 2004; Webster and Kirkpatrick, 2006; for a review, see Salmivalli, 2001), and heightened racial and gender prejudice (see Hunter et al., 1997 Hunter et al. 2011; Jordan et al., 2005; for a review, see also Aberson, Healey and Romero, 2001; Emler. 2001). Some researchers have suggested that these costs stem not from self-esteem itself, but from the *pursuit* of self-esteem (e.g., Crocker, 2002; Crocker and Park, 2003, 2004). Failure, or potential failure, experienced in the pursuit of self-esteem is regarded as a threat to a person's self-esteem goals and individuals can respond to these threats in potentially costly ways (see Crocker, 2002; Crocker and Park, 2003, 2004). In their review, Crocker and Park (2004) suggest that people may use drugs and alcohol in order to cope with failure. Individuals may also become more aggressive towards others because, in their pursuit of self-esteem, they come to view others as rivals. Finally, people may show prejudice towards others, depicting out-group members as doing more poorly than themselves, in an effort to recover self-esteem after a self-esteem threat. Such costs have prompted Crocker and Park (2004) to recommend that efforts to improve self-esteem should be abandoned.

In contrast to such views, other theorists have subsequently proposed that it is possible to pursue self-esteem in a way that ensures that the negative effects of high self-esteem are not incurred (see DuBois and Flay, 2004; Pyszczynski and Cox, 2004; Sheldon, 2004). While the individual theories proposed by these theorists differ, they are each underpinned by the same basic principle. This principle is that, if one takes the needs of others into consideration when one seeks self-esteem, the negative consequences associated with the pursuit may be avoided (see DuBois and Flay, 2004; Pyszczynski and Cox, 2004; Sheldon, 2004).

This study examined the immediate and medium-term impact on participants' self-esteem of a 10-day training programme aboard the sailing vessel the *Spirit of New Zealand* (or the *Spirit*). The investigation further sought to determine whether self-esteem could be improved over the course of the sail-training intervention without corresponding increases in a range of negative consequences which have been linked to high self-esteem (i.e., risky attitudes towards drug and alcohol use, physical and verbal aggression, and racial and gender bias). Three hypotheses were tested. The first hypothesis predicted that individuals participating in a 10-day developmental sail-training intervention aboard the *Spirit* would experience self-esteem increases between the first day of the voyage (T2) and the last day of the voyage (T3). The second hypothesis predicted that self-esteem improvements, made over the course of the intervention, would endure four to five months after the voyage (T4). The third hypothesis predicted that self-esteem increases observed would not be associated with corresponding increases in costs (i.e., risky attitudes towards drug and alcohol use, physical and verbal aggression, and racial and gender bias).

METHOD

Participants

One hundred and fifty-three people took part in this study. An intervention group comprised 100 trainees who undertook one of three 10-day voyages on the sail-training vessel, the Spirit of New Zealand. In this condition there were

52 males and 48 females. Each voyage was mixed-sex. Participants were aged between 14 and 18 years.[1] Intervention participants were recruited by the Spirit of Adventure Trust from a range of schools around New Zealand (Hylton, 2003; Lott, 2003). Trainees were comprised of a wide range of backgrounds. Some volunteered, and some were nominated by schools and outside agencies (e.g., the court system). Reasons for nomination were various. These included attempts to bolster the confidence of shy or withdrawn students, a desire to improve the drive of students lacking in motivation and as a reward for those doing well (see Basham, 2003). A non-intervention control group consisted of 53 secondary school students from two mixed-sex schools in the city of Dunedin, in New Zealand. This non-intervention sample contained 24 female and 29 male participants, aged between 15 and 18 years.

The 10-Day Developmental Voyage on the Spirit of New Zealand

The Spirit of New Zealand is a 45-metre, 3 masted Barquentine which sails the costal waters around New Zealand. Although an important part of the voyage entails 'Sail Training' (i.e., learning to sail a masted sailing ship), the core purpose of the voyage is to foster youth development (Leppington, 2003). The 10-day developmental voyage is demanding yet supportive. The weather is often inclement and seasickness is widespread. There are no showers and all participants take a daily 6 AM swim around the vessel. Shipboard life allows few opportunities for privacy and, once the vessel has set sail, little by way of exit an option. The voyage is organised so that none of the participants know each other beforehand (thus they cannot rely on pre-existing friendships). Cell phones, personal computers and other electrical equipment are not permitted on board. Neither is 'labelled' clothing. These latter factors help facilitate new friendships, equality of social status and similar levels of belonging at the start of the voyage.

The onboard programme emphasizes acceptance, support and self-efficacy. These qualities are imparted via group based processes (which invoke belonging, interdependence and cooperation), positive encouragement and the succesful completion of the many challenges encountered during the voyage (e.g., being away from home, making new friends, the daily 6 AM swim around the vessel, cooking, cleaning the toilets, climbing the rigging,

---

[1] Research examining a similar sample of adolescent trainees, undertaking the same developmental sail training programme on board the Spirit of New Zealand, revealed that less than five per cent of participants identified with an ethnic group other than New Zealand European (Grocott and Hunter, 2009). In view of this, the present study did not measure ethnic identity.

completing one's duties regardless of seasickness, tiredness, rolling ocean swells, or rough weather, working with others, living in a confined space, and eventually sailing the ship without help from the crew).

The core social group over the course of the voyage is the 'watch'. The watch is typically comprised of five males and five females. Voyage participants join their respective watch on the first day of the programmme. They then remain in this group throughout the voyage and work closely with one another in a variety of goal oriented activities. These processes promote group belonging, cohesion and mutual cooperation, which in turn foster respect and acceptance amongst group members (see Brown, 2000). Each day a different person is leader of their watch. Their job is to lead the watch in the various activities throughout the day, from cleaning the ship in the morning, to the final debriefing session in the evening. The watch leader is encouraged by the crew to ensure every member of the watch has a job to do when sailing or participating in any given activity.

After each activity a crew member debriefs watch members by discussing the activity just completed. Each evening the full day's events and activities are debriefed. Debriefing involves an introductory discussion (to prepare participants for any given activity), a discussion of what the activity itself entails, followed by debriefing to process the experience of the activity and what participants may gain from it. In addition to a member of the crew facilitating a final debrief at the conclusion of the day's activities, each watch leader of the day take a turn to talk about what they personally gained from the day, how well their watch worked together, what they liked or disliked, and pass on suggestions to others about ways of succeeding at the tasks set.

Integral to the voyage are the opportunities that participants have to learn through experience. The ship is divided up into four sail stations (foredeck, midships, mains, and rear). Each watch moves to a new station each day and learns the correct method of rasing of lowering the sails in question (this can only be achieved if all watch members cooperate). The rigging of the vessel has been purposely kept as simple as possible to ensure that participants, most of whom have never done any sailing, can learn the correct methods of manoeuvring the sails with a high chance of success. Indeed, ensuring that activities, whether setting a sail or other group based exercises, have every chance of success is an important part of the voyage programme, in so far as the successful completion of such activities is an important precursor to self-efficacy and self-esteem (Bandura, 2006; Gecas and Schwalbe, 1983).

Voyage participants take part in a number of activities over the course of a voyage. The timing of activities is often determined by the weather. A voyage does, however, follow a general pattern. On day one, trainees are given a talk on safety, day-to-day shipboard procedure (e.g., safety harness must be worn during rough weather, night sailing, traversing the bowsprit, climbing the rigging), presented with wet weather gear (jackets and leggings) and assigned a bunk in a single-sex, cramped communal dorm. Procedures for dealing with emergencies are emphasized. Trainees also receive a tour of the ship and a rundown of the sail station method used to sail the vessel.

Days two to four normally consists of activities set up to promote cooperation within and between the respective watches. This is achieved by a series of activities that will only be successful if the members of the watch cooperate. Thus, for example in one activity called 'Spiders web' a 'web' of rope is tied into the rigging of the ship. This web contains ten gaps. Each member of the watch must pass through a different gap in the web without touching the ropes. Some of the gaps are above head height to add challenge to the exercise, and to encourage cooperation for successful completion of the task. During these first few days of the voyage general safety features of the vessel are discussed along with correct response in an emergency situation. For this part of the voyage there is a 'hands on hands' approach from the crew. That is, the crew are actively involved in demonstrating and assisting with sail handling, and are fully involved with other watch activities.

During days five to eight there is a continuation of cooperative group activities, social support and success. Here the emphasis is on achievable tasks within watches, and as a complete crew. Activities are varied, ranging from tramping, sailing small boats, barbeques ashore, and inflatable raft paddling races, as well as sailing the ship. For the first part of this phase the crew adopt a 'hands on' approach where direction and assistance are given when needed. This changes to a 'hands off' approach around day seven. During this period voyage participants are encouraged to use their watch as a resource to solve problems, rather than relying on crew input, while at the same time handling sail and other watch activities.

The eight days of fostering acceptance, social support and efficacy (by positive reinforcement, facilitating success by having achievable activities, cooperative group activities, and discussing effective leadership) leads to what is termed 'trainee day' on day nine. Trainee day is where the voyage participants take over all aspects of running the ship for the day. The previous night the voyage participants elect their own Captain, Mate, Navigators, Engineers, Cooks, and Watch Leaders. This is an integral part of the voyage programme, and is one which is emphasised as a goal during the earlier part of the voyage. It is an opportunity for the voyage participants to use newly acquired skills and pool their knowledge of the ship rather than asking for assistance from crew members. In the evening after trainee day awards and certificates are presented to each participant. The vessel is usually alongside the wharf by 7 am the following morning where trainees (often after a tearful farewell) depart and travel back to their homes.

Design

The core design of the study was mixed model. Time of self-esteem measurement was a within subjects variable (i.e., the self-esteem scale was presented to both intervention and non-intervention participants at T1, T2, T3, and T4). Condition (i.e., intervention vs. non-intervention) and gender (i.e., male vs. female) were between subjects variables. To determine whether self-esteem increases were associated with costs, intervention (but not non-intervention) participants' attitudes towards drug and alcohol use, physical and verbal aggression, and racial and gender bias were also assessed at T1, T2, T3, and T4.[2]

Materials

Self-esteem. The short form of the Self-Description Questionnaire (SDQ III) as designed by Marsh and colleagues (see Marsh et al., 1985; see also Marsh and Byrne, 1993; Marsh and O'Neill, 1984; Marsh et al., 1986a,b; Marsh and Richards, 1990) was administered. The scale consists of 13 items in total, measuring global (or general) self-esteem and 12 domains of self-esteem. The content of the subscales are Math: 'I am quite good at mathematics'; General School Work: 'I have trouble with most school subjects'; Religion/Spirituality: 'Spiritual/religious beliefs make my life better and me a better person'; Global Self: 'Overall, I don't have much respect for myself'; Honesty: 'I am a very honest person'; Opposite Sex Relations: 'I have lots of friends of the opposite sex'; Same Sex Relations: 'I make friends easily with members of the same sex'; Parental Relations: 'My parents understand me';

---

[2] The schools from which the non-intervention participants were drawn were unwilling to have students respond to the questions assessing attitudes towards drug and alcohol use, physical and verbal aggression, and racial and gender bias. Costs were, therefore, not examined among non-intervention participants. The schools' decision appeared to be a consequence of two issues. The first pertained to reluctance due to the potentially sensitive nature of the questions asked. The second concerned time constraints.

Physical Appearance: 'I dislike the way I look'; Physical Ability: 'I am a good athlete'; Verbal Ability: 'I have a poor vocabulary'; Emotional Stability: 'I worry a lot'; Problem Solving Ability: 'I am good at combining ideas in ways that others have not tried'. Responses are scored on 8-point Likert scales (1-Definitely False, 8-Definitely True). Five of the thirteen items in the scale are phrased in the negative. Higher scores denote higher self-esteem (Marsh and Richards, 1990). Reliability analysis of the SDQ III, over the experimental period from T2 to T3, revealed that the scale demonstrates both internal reliability (Cronbach's alpha = .71, n = 141) and test-retest reliability (r = .79, n = 140).

Drug and alcohol use. Participants completed six single items devised by Gibbons et al. (2004), tapping behavioural willingness (BW) to use drugs and drink alcohol and behavioural intention (BI) to use drugs and drink alcohol. The content of the items assessing behavioural willingness to use drugs are 'Suppose that you were with a group of friends and there were some drugs that you could have if you wanted (1) Would you be willing to take some and use it?; (2) Would you be willing to use enough to get high?'. Items evaluating behavioural willingness to use alcohol are 'Suppose that you were with a group of friends and there was some alcohol that you could have if you wanted (3) Would you be willing to take some and drink it?; (4) Would you be willing to get drunk?'. The content of the items measuring behavioural intention to use drugs and drink alcohol are (5) 'I plan to take drugs in the next year; (6) I plan to drink alcohol in the next year'. Responses were recorded on 8-point Likert scales (1-Definitely False, 8-Definitely True). Higher scores denote greater willingness or intention to take drugs and drink alcohol. Reliability analysis over the experimental period from T2 to T3 showed that the scales demonstrate both internal (Cronbach's alpha = .90, n = 86) and test-retest reliability (r = .77, n = 86).

Physical and verbal aggression. Scales from Buss and Perry's (1992) aggression questionnaire were administered to tap physical and verbal aggression in the present study. The physical aggression scale is comprised of nine items, and the verbal aggression scale, five. An example of a scale item assessing physical aggression is 'Given enough provocation, I may hit another person'. An example of an item measuring verbal aggression is 'I often find myself disagreeing with people'. Responses are recorded on a 5-point Likert scale (1-Extremely Uncharacteristic of me, 5-Extremely Characteristic of me). Higher scores denote higher physical and verbal aggression. Reliability analysis of the physical and verbal aggression scales over the intervention period (i.e., from T2 to T3), revealed that the scales demonstrate acceptable levels of internal reliability (Cronbach's alphas: physical aggression = .77, n = 84; verbal aggression = .63, n = 84) and test-retest reliability (physical aggression r = .78, n = 84; verbal aggression r = .69, n = 84).

Racial and gender bias. The measures of racial and gender bias are a variant of the zero-sum allocation tasks used by Amiot and Bourhis (2005) and Hodson, Dovidio and Esses (2003) to investigate intergroup bias. In order to assess racial bias, participants were asked to divide $10,000 between a White European individual and an Asian individual.[3] To examine gender bias, participants were asked to divide $10,000 between a male and female. The pair was identified as Jack and Emily. These names topped a list of 50 in a 2003 UK Baby Centre survey of popular boys' and girls' names ("Top UK Baby Names 2003", 2003). In both the racial bias task and the gender bias task participants were advised that they could allocate as much or as little to any one person, as long as the overall amount did not total more than $10,000.[4] Tests of the racial and gender bias zero-sum allocation task, over the experimental period from T2 to T3, revealed that the scales demonstrate test-retest reliability (racial bias r = .62, n = 80; gender bias r = .62, n = 81).

Procedure

Intervention and non-intervention participants completed the short form of the SDQ III three to four weeks prior to the first day of the sailing programme (T1), on the first day of the programme (T2), on the last day of the programme (T3), and between four and five months after the final day of the programme (T4). The experimental period between T2 and T3 spanned 10 days. Ten days is the standard duration of youth development voyages set by the Spirit of Adventure Trust ("Spirit of Adventure Trust", 2005). Intervention participants also responded to the Behavioural Willingness and Intention to use Drugs and Drink Alcohol scales, the Physical and Verbal Aggression scales, and the Zero-Sum Allocation measures of Racial and Gender Prejudice at T1, T2, T3, and T4. Intervention and non-intervention participants' self-esteem was assessed at T1 to ensure that intervention participants' self-esteem scores were not lower than usual at T2 (i.e., on the first day of the voyage). Trainees may

---

[3] New Zealand has a long and enduring history of prejudice against individuals of Asian descent (for reviews, see McLennan, Ryan, and Spoonley, 2000; Spoonley, 1988).
[4] The zero-sum allocation tasks are valid in the sense that a 50-50 distribution of the money indicates an absence of prejudice. An unequal distribution of funds, on the other hand, denotes racial or gender bias.

have experienced a transitory decrease in self-esteem as they embarked on a demanding course, in an unfamiliar environment (see Marsh et al., 1986b; see also Hattie et al., 1997 for further discussion of the benefits of collecting pretest measures).

Intervention and non-intervention participants' self-esteem was examined at T4 in order to determine whether intervention participants' self-esteem scores remained elevated four to five months after the intervention. The follow-up measures also helped to establish that any self-esteem increases observed immediately after programme completion, were not simply attributable to a phenomenon known as 'postgroup euphoria', or PGE (see Marsh et al., 1986a,b).

Simply put, PGE refers to the feelings of elation experienced immediately after a concentrated period spent in a group setting (Marsh et al., 1986b). If present, this sense of euphoria can cause self-esteem to be temporarily elevated. If self-esteem improvements documented on the final day of the voyage (T3) were a consequence of PGE, then intervention participants' self-esteem would have returned to pre-voyage levels when assessed four to five months after the last day of the programme (T4 [see Marsh et al., 1986a]).

RESULTS

The data from participants from all three voyages was combined. At the outset, the final analysis was comprised of 89 intervention participants and 53 non-intervention participants. Overall, there were 75 female participants and 67 males. Criteria for inclusion in the final analysis required that participants in both the intervention and the non-intervention group had responded to a minimum of three of the four (T1, T2, T3, T4) questionnaires. Where data was missing from individual questionnaires, the value was recoded as the mean for the overall sample at that time. The number of participants who completed the questionnaire at each time varied, as did the number of participants included in each of the analyses.

Intervention and Non-Intervention Participants' Self-Esteem

To assess self-esteem three to four weeks prior (T1), on the first day (T2), on the last day (T3), and four to five months following the voyage (T4), a 2 (condition: intervention vs. non-intervention) x 4 (time of self-esteem measurement: T1, T2, T3, T4) mixed model ANOVA was conducted.[5] Condition was a between subjects factors. Time of self-esteem measurement was a within subjects factor. All cell means are presented in Table 1.

The only significant effect to emerge, with an alpha level of .05, was the expected interaction found between condition and time of self-esteem measurement $F(1, 89) = 5.00$, $p < .03$. Planned comparisons (using repeated measures t-tests) showed that intervention participants experienced an increase in self-esteem over the course of the 10-day voyage from T2 to T3 $t(87) = 5.31$, $p < .0005$. This effect was also significant when using Dunn's (Bonferroni t) test to control for the family-wise and error rate (critical alpha value = 3.31, $p < .01$).[6]

---

[5] A preliminary analysis in the form of a 3 (voyage: 1, 2, 3) x 2 (gender: male v female) x 2 (condition: intervention v non intervention) x 13 (self-esteem domains: Math, Religion/Spirituality, Global Self, Honesty, Opposite Sex Relations, Same Sex Relations, Parental Relations, Physical Appearance, Physical Ability, Verbal Ability, Emotional Stability, General School Work, Problem Solving Ability) x 4 (time of self-esteem measurement: T1, T2, T3, T4) mixed model analysis of variance (ANOVA) was conducted. No relevant significant main or interaction effects were found as a function of voyage, gender, or self-esteem domain. For ease of presentation, voyage and gender were excluded from further analyses. As a result also, overall self-esteem scores, rather than individual domain-level scores, are reported in subsequent analyses.

[6] One criticism which may be leveled at the present study concerns the fact that attitudes towards drug and alcohol use, physical and verbal aggression, and racial and gender bias were not examined among non-intervention participants. It is possible that responding to questionnaires assessing these negative attitudes and behaviours, somehow caused intervention participants to experience the self-esteem increases over the course of the 10-day period, from T2 to T3. To test this unlikely possibility, an independent manipulation check was conducted with a sample of 72 undergraduate students from the University of Otago. The manipulation check group was comprised of 53 females and 19 males, with a mean age of 20 years. Participants' self-esteem, attitudes towards drug and alcohol use, physical and verbal aggression, and racial and gender bias were assessed on two occasions, once on the first day of the introductory section of a semester-long university Psychology course (T2) and again 10 days later, on the final day of the introductory segment of the course (T3). To assess whether there were any differences in the self-esteem of participants in the intervention group and participants in the manipulation check group at T2, a one-way between subjects ANOVA was conducted. No significant differences were found F(1, 161) = 2.03, p > .15. That is, there were no disparities between the self-esteem of participants in the intervention group (M = 73.11, SD = 9.56) and participants in the manipulation check group (M = 71.15, SD = 7.49). To determine whether the manipulation check participants' self-esteem changed between T2 and T3, a repeated measures within subjects ANOVA was carried out. No effect emerged F(1, 71) = 1.25, p > .26. That is, participants' self-esteem was unaltered from T2 (M = 71.15, SD = 7.49) to T3 (M = 71.81, SD = 6.66). The negative outcomes associated with high self-esteem were similarly unchanged over the 10 day period, from T2 to T3. Finally, analyses examining age and sex as either co-variates or between subjects factors, showed that neither of the variables had consequences for self-esteem, as assessed at T2 and T3.

Table 1. Intervention and Non-Intervention Participants' Mean Self-Esteem Scores at T1, T2, T3 and T4

	Mean Score (SD)			
Condition	Time 1	Time 2	Time 3	Time 4
Intervention	73.05^a (9.22)	73.60^b (9.93)	76.99^c*** (9.57)	76.60^d (8.54)
Non-intervention	72.23^e (10.34)	72.13^f (8.31)	71.10^g (8.16)	71.69^h (12.72)

Note. Higher scores denote higher levels of self-esteem.
$^a n = 53$. $^b n = 88$. $^c n = 89$. $^d n = 56$. $^e n = 52$. $^f n = 53$. $^g n = 51$. $^h n = 52$.
***Increase in self-esteem from T2-T3 $p < .0005$.

Intervention participants' self-esteem did not change from T1 to T2 $t(51) = .49, p > .63$. Any changes from the first day of the intervention (T2) to the last day of the intervention (T3), therefore, cannot be explained on the basis of self-esteem being restored after an artificial decrease at T2. Similarly, intervention participants' self-esteem did not change between T3, the final day of the voyage, and T4, four to five months after the last day of the intervention $t(55) = .24, p > .80$. The self-esteem increases that trainees experienced over the 10-day sail-training period from T2 to T3 were, therefore, still in effect four to five months after the last day of the voyage (T4). Participants in the non-intervention control group experienced no self-esteem change between T2 and T3, $t(50) = 1.61, p < .11$. Non-intervention participants' self-esteem was similarly unaltered between T1 and T2 $t(51) = .02, p > .98$ and between T3 and T4 $t(50) = .38, p > .70$.

Intervention Participants' Attitudes towards Drug and Alcohol Use

To assess potential changes in attitudes towards drug and alcohol use over the course of the voyage, a 6 (attitude type: 1. willing to take drugs, 2. willing to get high, 3. willing to drink, 4. willing to get drunk, 5. intention to take drugs in next year, 6. intention to drink in next year) x 4 (time of attitude measurement: T1, T2, T3, T4) repeated measures ANOVA was conducted.[7] Cell means may be seen in Table 2.

The only effect to emerge, using an alpha level of .05, was for attitude type $F(1, 36) = 47.60$, $p < .001$. Post hoc comparisons using repeated measures t-tests revealed higher scores overall, for willingness to drink ($M = 6.19$, $SD = 2.09$), willingness to get drunk ($M = 4.47$, $SD = 2.65$), and intention to drink alcohol ($M = 6.43$, $SD = 2.13$) than for willingness to take drugs ($M = 2.01$, $SD = 1.91$), willingness to get high ($M = 1.97$, $SD = 1.88$), and intention to take drugs ($M = 1.69$, $SD = 1.59$ [all p's <.001]).

Table 2. Intervention Participants' Mean Scores for Attitudes towards Drug and Alcohol Use at T1, T2, T3, and T4

	Mean Score (SD)			
Attitude Type	Time 1[a]	Time 2[b]	Time 3[c]	Time 4[d]
Willing to take drugs	1.81 (1.58)	2.17 (1.99)	1.92 (1.98)	2.17 (2.10)
Willing to get high	1.75 (1.46)	2.14 (2.13)	1.89 (1.91)	2.08 (2.03)
Willing to drink	6.11 (1.77)	6.06 (2.11)	5.89 (2.48)	6.69 (2.01)
Willing to get drunk	4.33 (2.40)	4.36 (2.66)	4.61 (2.75)	4.56 (2.79)
Intention to take drugs	1.67 (1.53)	1.86 (1.81)	1.50 (1.46)	1.75 (1.56)
Intention to drink	5.97 (2.25)	6.17 (2.32)	6.42 (2.16)	7.17 (1.78)

Note. Higher scores denote greater willingness and intention to take drugs and alcohol. [a]$n = 51$. [b]$n = 86$. [c]$n = 86$. [d]$n = 55$.

Table 3. Intervention Participants' Mean Physical and Verbal Aggression Scores at T1, T2, T3, and T4

	Mean Score (SD)			
Aggression Type	Time 1	Time 2	Time 3	Time 4
Physical aggression	19.64[a] (6.39)	19.25[b] (5.83)	19.31[c] (6.42)	19.69[d] (6.43)
Verbal aggression	15.47[e] (3.47)	15.67[f] (3.80)	15.03[g] (4.32)	13.50[h] (3.71)

Note. Higher scores denote greater physical and verbal aggression. [a]$n = 48$. [b]$n = 84$. [c]$n = 84$. [d]$n = 55$. [e]$n = 51$. [f]$n = 84$. [g]$n = 84$. [h]$n = 55$.

---

[7]Preliminary analyses failed to reveal any gender or voyage effects. Subsequently, for ease of presentation, these variables were excluded from further analyses. Note also that in light of the preliminary nature of this investigation, we examined the responses to each question separately.

Table 4. Mean Sums of Money Allocated to European and Asian Targets by Intervention Participants at T1, T2, T3, and T4

Target of bias	Time 1[a]	Time 2[b]	Time 3[c]	Time 4[d]
European (Ingroup)	5052.78 (1166.55)	5347.22 (969.68)	5144.44 (1448.04)	5283.33 (1071.05)
Asian (Outgroup)	4947.22 (1166.55)	4652.78 (969.68)	4855.56 (1448.04)	4716.67 (1071.05)

Note. Higher scores denote greater racial bias.
[a]$n = 52$. [b]$n = 81$. [c]$n = 80$. [d]$n = 54$.

No differences were found between willingness to drink, willingness to get drunk, and intention to drink alcohol or between willingness to take drugs, willingness to get high, and intention to take drugs.

Intervention Participants' Physical and Verbal Aggression

To examine potential changes in physical and verbal aggression over the course of the intervention a 2 (aggression type: physical, verbal) x 4 (time of aggression measurement: T1, T2, T3, T4) repeated measures ANOVA was conducted.[8] Cell means may be seen in Table 3.

The only effect to emerge, using an alpha level of .05, was a main effect found for aggression type $F(1, 34) = 27.29$, $p < .001$. Overall, scores for physical aggression ($M = 19.47$, $SD = 4.87$) were higher than scores for verbal aggression ($M = 14.92$, $SD = 3.73$).

Intervention Participants' Racial Bias

To assess potential changes in monetary allocations to racial ingroup and outgroup members over the course of the intervention, a 2 (target of allocation bias: European, Asian) x 4 (time of bias measurement: T1, T2, T3, T4) repeated measures ANOVA was conducted. Cell means may be seen in Table 4.[9] There were no main or interaction effects.

---

[8]Preliminary analyses failed to reveal any gender or voyage effects. Subsequently, for ease of presentation, these variables were excluded from further analyses.
[9]Preliminary analyses failed to reveal any gender or voyage effects. Subsequently, for ease of presentation, these variables were excluded from further analyses.

Table 5. Mean Sums of Money Allocated to Men and Women Targets by Intervention Participants at T1, T2, T3, and T4

	Target of bias	Time 1[a]	Time 2[b]	Time 3[c]	Time 4[d]
	(Ingroup)	4678.57 (822.92)	4928.57 (267.26)	5000.00 (.00)	4857.14 (363.14)
Men	(Outgroup)	5321.43 (822.92)	5071.43 (267.26)	5000.00 (.00)	5142.86 (363.14)
	(Ingroup)	5045.45 (213.20)	5000.05 (.21)	4999.95 (.21)	5142.85 (636.13)
Women	(Outgroup)	4954.55 (213.20)	4999.95 (.21)	5000.05 (.21)	4857.15 (636.13)

Note. Higher scores denote greater gender bias.
[a]$n = 52$. [b]$n = 81$. [c]$n = 81$. [d]$n = 54$.

Intervention Participants' Gender Bias

To examine potential changes in monetary allocations to gender ingroup and outgroup members over the course of the intervention, a 2 (gender: male v female) x 2 (target of allocation bias: men, women) x 4 (time of bias measurement: T1, T2, T3, T4) mixed model ANOVA was conducted.[10] Cell means are presented in Table 5.

There were no significant main or interaction effects.

DISCUSSION

Three hypotheses were tested in the present investigation. The first hypothesis predicted that individuals participating in a 10-day developmental sail-training intervention aboard the *Spirit* would experience self-esteem increases between the first day of the voyage (T2) and the last day of the voyage (T3). The second hypothesis predicted that self-esteem improvements, made over the course of the intervention, would endure four to five months after the voyage (T4). The third hypothesis predicted that self-esteem increases

---

[10] A preliminary analysis failed to reveal any voyage effects. Subsequently, for ease of presentation, this variable was excluded from further analyses.

observed would not be associated with corresponding increases in negative outcomes (i.e., risky attitudes towards drug and alcohol use, physical and verbal aggression, and racial and gender bias). Support was found for each hypothesis.

With regard to the first hypothesis, those participants who undertook the voyage experienced self-esteem increases between the first (T2) and the last day of the voyage (T3).[11] With regard to the second hypothesis, there was no significant change in participants' self-esteem between the last day of the sail-training intervention (T3), and four to five months after the last day of the intervention (T4). Thus, increases in self-esteem found over the course of the voyage were enduring in the medium term. With regard to the third hypothesis , the self-esteem increases in the current study were not linked with corresponding increases in negative outcomes. These results indicate that increased self-esteem is not, as has been suggested, necessarily associated with negative outcomes such as elevated drug and alcohol use (see Karatzias et al., 2001; Scheier et al., 2000), amplified physical and verbal aggression (for a review, see Salmivalli, 2001), and increased racial (Jordan et al., 2005) or gender bias (Hunter et al., 1997; Jordan et al., 2005, see also Hunter 1998). In this respect, the present findings are consistent with the theory that self-esteem can be attained without negative consequences (see DuBois and Flay, 2004; Pyszczynski and Cox, 2004; Sheldon, 2004).

An application of theories of self-esteem development to the processes involved in the sail-training intervention may afford insight into the programme practices that lead to self-esteem improvement in the current study (see Emler. 2001; Klint, 1999). The Jamesian Discrepancy Model (James, 1890/1981) and Cooley's 'looking-glass-self' theory of self-esteem development (Cooley, 1902) both provide plausible accounts of how self-esteem may have been increased (see Emler. 2001). According to the Jamesian Discrepancy Model, the gap between a person's goals and his or her achievements is seminal in determining the level of an individual's self-esteem (James, 1890/1981). Those who have a favourable view of the self in areas in which they wish to succeed will have high self-esteem. Those whose ambitions are unattainable, thus causing a mismatch between their goals and their perceived achievements, will suffer from low self-esteem (see also, Crocker and Luhtanen, 2003; Crocker, Luhtanen, Cooper, and Bouvrette, 2003; Crocker et al., 2002; Crocker and Wolfe, 2001; Harter, 1990a,b; Harter,

---

[11] Recall that a preliminary analysis in the results revealed no significant differences between global and domain-specific self-esteem or between separate self-esteem domains. As a result, the term 'self-esteem' refers to both global and domain-specific self-esteem.

1993; Harter, 1996; Harter, 1998; Harter, 2003; Harter and Marold, 1994; Harter and Whitesell, 2001; Luhtanen and Crocker, 2005). According to the looking-glass-self theory, close others provide 'social mirrors' that reflect back the others' views of an individual (Cooley, 1902). A person's perception of these views is then used to assess their own merit (see also, Emler, 2001; Harter, 1990a,b; Harter, 1993; Harter, 2003; Harter and Marold, 1994; Harter, Stocker, and Robinson, 1996). Others who show respect and appreciation will prompt a person to internalise a positive view of the self, while those who fail to provide positive feedback will lead a person to internalise a negative view of the self (Harter, 2003; see also, Brinthaupt and Lipka, 2002). Research suggests that the Jamesian Discrepancy Model and Cooley's looking-glass-self theory operate in tandem to explain self-esteem change (for reviews, see Harter, 1990b; Harter, 1996; Harter and Marold, 1994).

There are two ways in which the Jamesian theory can account for self-esteem increases among participants, over the course of an intervention. The first concerns participants' sense of achievement (Emler. 2001). The *Spirit* 10-day programme is structured so that trainees have the best possible chance of succeeding. The second concerns the process of bringing participants' aims into line with their abilities. An intervention may achieve this in two ways. The first is to modify the relative value placed on objectives (Emler. 2001). *Spirit* voyages focus on improving skills across a range of areas, with equal importance placed on performance in each area. The second is by ensuring that individuals set realistic goals. It is important that people set objectives that are in line with their own abilities, rather than competing with others (Emler. 2001). At the voyage's outset, *Spirit* trainees are asked to set targets which, although challenging, are attainable. There is also a clear focus on cooperative teamwork, with competition between trainees de-emphasised.

There is one critical way in which Cooley's looking-glass-self theory can account for self-esteem change among participants over the course of an intervention. Exposing programme participants to the positive appraisals of others plays a key role in bringing about self-esteem increases (Emler. 2001). On a *Spirit* voyage, participants are removed from external influences for the duration of the programme. The setting thus presents a unique opportunity to limit trainees' exposure to potentially negative feedback. By maintaining conditions in which trainees share relatively equal status and work together as a group to achieve goals, the sailing programme's design maximises the likelihood that participants will receive the approval of fellow trainees.

The findings showing that voyage participants self-esteem remained high 4-5 months following the last day of the voyage are consistent with the results reported by Grocott and Hunter (2009). One reason for the maintenance of high self-esteem 4-5 months after the completion of the sailing programme is possibly due to the fact that individuals acquired a sense of self-efficacy as a consequence of the skills that they mastered over the course of the voyage (see Bandura, Caprara, Barbaranelli, Gerbino, and Pastorelli, 2003; Gecas, and Schwalbe, 1983; Hunter et al. 2010). This sense of their own competency and ability to exert control over the outcomes of situations may have been transferred to participants' everyday lives.

Recall that DuBois and Flay (2004), Pyszczynski and Cox (2004), and Sheldon (2004) contend that it is the way in which self-esteem is *pursued* which determines whether the acquisition of high self-esteem is free of costs.[12] The authors each separately emphasise the importance of setting and achieving objectives. One's attempts at skill development should, however, be directed towards fostering positive relationships with others and meeting the needs of others, rather than an individual focusing on him or herself when seeking to accomplish goals. These theories may afford insight into the shipboard practices which contributed to self-esteem improvement without negative consequences in the current investigation. As discussed earlier, an emphasis on achieving goals through cooperation and teamwork underpins the 10-day *Spirit* training programme. This may explain the cost free self-esteem increases found in the present study.

Further research is clearly necessary in order to establish how self-esteem is increased and maintained without costs, as a consequence of voyage participation. If studies isolate the processes that contribute to the sustained and positive attainment of self-esteem, then sail-training or other educational interventions may be tailored to maximise their efficiency.

A weakness of the present study concerns the evaluation of costs (i.e., approval of drug and alcohol use, physical and verbal aggression, and racial and gender bias) associated with high self-esteem. Evidence of these costs among control participants was not examined. The fact, however, that the costs have previously been linked to self-esteem increases (see Hunter et al., 1997 Hunter et al. in press; Jordan et al., 2005; Karatzias et al., 2001; Salmivalli, 2001; Scheier et al., 2000) and that control participants' self-esteem did not elevate over the course of the study period, renders it unlikely that non-intervention participants would have displayed increases in these negative outcomes. Inclusion of our manipulation check confirmed this. Future research

---

[12] In the current study, high self-esteem is treated as a relative rather than an absolute state. The terms 'self-esteem increase' and 'high self-esteem' are thus used interchangeably.

should, however, assess the costs among the control participants rather than evaluating them separately.

The finding that adolescents' self-esteem increased, without corresponding increases in costs, has considerable implications for current theory and practice. Recall that some theorists (e.g., Crocker and Park, 2004) have proposed that efforts to improve self-esteem should be abandoned. Although other theorists have maintained that it is possible to elevate self-esteem without corresponding costs (e.g., DuBois and Flay, 2004; Pyszczynski and Cox, 2004; Sheldon, 2004), until now this claim has not been empirically assessed. Given the host of benefits associated with high self-esteem (Baumeister et al., 2003; see also DuBois and Flay, 2004; Leary, 1999b) and similarly numerous negative outcomes linked with low self-esteem (Emler, 2001; see also Harter, 2003), the findings from the present study show that certain kinds of intervention designed to foster increased self-esteem are clearly worthwhile.

REFERENCES

Aberson, C. L., Healy, M., and Romero, V. (2000). Ingroup bias and self-esteem: a meta-analysis. *Personality and Social Psychology Review, 4*(2), 157-173.

Akrami, N., Ekehammar, B., and Araya, T. (2000). Classical and modern racial prejudice: a study of attitudes toward immigrants in Sweden. *European Journal of Social Psychology, 30,* 521-532.

Amiot, C. E., and Bourhis, R. Y. (2005). Ideological beliefs as determinants of discrimination in positive and negative outcome distributions. *European Journal of Social Psychology, 35,* 581-598.

Bandura, A. (2006). Adolescent development from an agentic perspective (pp. 1-43). In F. Pajares and T. Urdan (Eds.), *Self-efficacy beliefs of adolescents.* Greenwich, CT: Information Age Publishing.

Bandura, A., Caprara, G. V., Barbaranelli, C., Gerbino, M., and Pastorelli, C. (2003). Role of affective self-regulatory efficacy in diverse spheres of psychosocial functioning. *Child Development, 74*(3), 769-782.

Basham, C. (2003). A teacher's view. In T. Duder, and K. Thompson (Eds.), *Spirit of youth: thirty years of the Spirit of Adventure trust* (pp. 78-80). Auckland: Exisle Publishing Limited.

Baumeister, R. F., Bushman, B. J., and Campbell, W. K. (2000). Self-esteem, narcissism, and aggression: does violence result from low self-esteem or from threatened egotism? *Current Directions in Psychological Science, 9*(1), 26-29.

Baumeister, R. F., Campbell, J. D., Krueger, J. I., and Vohs, K. D. (2003). Does high self-esteem cause better performance, interpersonal success, happiness, or healthier lifestyles? *Psychological Science in the Public Interest, 4,* 1-44.

Baumeister, R. F., Smart, L., and Boden, J. M. (1996). Relation of threatened egotism to violence and aggression: the dark side of high self-esteem. *Psychological Review, 103*(1), 5-33.

Beane, J. A., and Lipka, R. P. (1986). *Self-Concept, Self-Esteem, and the Curriculum.* New York: Teachers College Press.

Bjorkqvist, K. (1994). Sex differences in physical, verbal, and indirect aggression: a review of recent research. *Sex Roles: A Journal of Research, 30*(3-4), 177-189.

Breckell, G. (2003). Taking risks. In T. Duder, and K. Thompson (Eds.), *Spirit of youth: thirty years of the Spirit of Adventure trust* (pp. 90-92). Auckland: Exisle Publishing Limited.

Brinthaupt, T. M., and Lipka, R. P. (2002). Understanding early adolescent self and identity: an introduction. In T. M. Brinthaupt, and R. P. Lipka (Eds.), *Understanding early adolescent self and identity. Applications and interventions* (pp.1-21). New York: State University of New York Press.

Brown, J. D. (1998). *The self.* Boston: McGraw-Hill.

Brown, J. D., and Dutton, K. A. (1995). Truth and consequences: the costs and benefits of accurate self-knowledge. *Personality and Social Psychology Bulletin, 21*(12), 1288-1296.

Brown, J. D., and McGill, K. L. (1989). The cost of good fortune: when positive life events produce negative health consequences. *Journal of Personality and Social Psychology, 57*(6), 1103-1110.

Brown, R. (2000). Group Processes. Oxford: Blackwell.

Bushman, B. J., and Baumeister, R. F. (1998). Threatened egotism, narcissism, self-esteem, and direct and displaced aggression: does self-love or self-hate lead to violence? *Journal of Personality and Social Psychology, 75*(1), 219-229.

Buss, A. H., and Perry, M. (1992). The aggression questionnaire. *Journal of Personality and Social Psychology, 63*(3), 452-459.

Byrne, B. M. (1988a). Measuring adolescent self-concept: factorial validity and equivalency of the SDQ III across gender. *Multivariate Behavioural Research, 23,* 361-375.

Byrne, B. M. (1988b). The self-description questionnaire III: testing for equivalent factorial validity across ability. *Educational and Psychological Measurement, 48,* 397-406.

Byrne, B. M. (1996). *Measuring self-concept across the lifespan: issues and instrumentation.* Washington: American Psychological Association.

Campbell, J. D. (1990). Self-esteem and clarity of the self-concept. *Journal of Personality and Social Psychology, 59*(3), 538-549.

Campbell, J. D., and Lavallee, L. F. (1993). Who am I? The role of self-concept confusion in understanding the behaviour of people with low self-esteem. In R. F. Baumeister (Ed.), *Self-Esteem: The Puzzle of Low Self-Regard* (pp. 3-20). New York: Plenum Press.

Chan, D. W. (1997). Self-concept domains and global self-worth among Chinese adolescents in Hong Kong. *Personality and Individual Differences, 22*(4), 511-520.

Cooley, C. H. (1902). *Human nature and the social order.* New York: Charles Scribner's Sons.

Cozzarelli, C. (1993). Personality and self-efficacy as predictors of coping with abortion. *Journal of Personality and Social Psychology,* 65(6), 1224-1236.

Crane, D., Hattie, J., and Houghton, S. (1997). Goal setting and the adventure experience. *Australian Journal of Psychology, 49*(1), 6-13.

Crocker, J. (1993). Memory for information about others: effects of self-esteem and performance feedback. *Journal of Research in Personality, 27,* 35-48.

Crocker, J. (2002). The costs of seeking self-esteem. *Journal of Social Issues, 58*(3), 597-615.

Crocker, J., and Luhtanen, R. (1990). Collective self-esteem and ingroup bias. *Journal Of Personality and Social Psychology, 58*(1), 60-67.

Crocker, J., and Luhtanen, R. K. (2003). Level of self-esteem and contingencies of self-worth: unique effects on academic, social and financial problems in college students. *Personality and Social Psychology Bulletin, 29*(6), 701-712.

Crocker, J., Luhtanen, R. K., Cooper, M. L., and Bouvrette, A. (2003). Contingencies of self-worth in college students: theory and measurement. *Journal of Personality and Social Psychology, 85*(5), 894-908.

Crocker, J., and Park, L. E. (2003). Seeking self-esteem: construction, maintenance, and protection of self-worth. In M. R. Leary, and J. P. Tangney (Eds.), *Handbook of Self and Identity* (pp. 291-313). New York: The Guilford Press.

Crocker, J., and Park, L. E. (2004). The costly pursuit of self-esteem. *Psychological Bulletin, 130*(3), 392-414.

Crocker, J., Sommers, S. R., and Luhtanen, R. K. (2002). Hopes dashed and dreams fulfilled: contingencies of self-worth and graduate school admissions. *Personality and Social Psychology Bulletin, 28*(9), 1275-1286.

Crocker, J., Thompson, L. L., McGraw, K. M., and Ingerman, C. (1987). Downward comparison, prejudice, and evaluations of others: effects of self-esteem and threat. *Journal of Personality and Social Psychology, 52*(5), 907-916.

Crocker, J., and Wolfe, C. T. (2001). Contingencies of self-worth. *Psychological Review, 108*(3), 593-623.

Culpan, A. (2003). To be who you want to be. In T. Duder, and K. Thompson (Eds.), *Spirit of youth: thirty years of the Spirit of Adventure trust* (pp. 115-117). Auckland: Exisle Publishing Limited.

Dijksterhuis, A. (2004). I like myself but I don't know why: enhancing implicit self-esteem by subliminal evaluative conditioning. *Journal of Personality and Social Psychology, 86*(2), 345-355.

Dillman, D. A. (2000). *Mail and internet surveys: the tailored design method.* New York: John Wiley and Sons, Inc.

Di Paula, A., and Campbell, J. D. (2002). Self-esteem and persistence in the face of failure. *Journal of Personality and Social Psychology, 83*(3), 711-724.

Dobson-Smith, R. (2003). A life-changing experience. In T. Duder, and K. Thompson (Eds.), *Spirit of youth: thirty years of the Spirit of Adventure trust* (pp. 118-119). Auckland: Exisle Publishing Limited.

Dodgson, P. G., and Wood, J. V. (1998). Self-esteem and the cognitive accessibility of strengths and weaknesses after failure. *Journal of Personality and Social Personality, 75*(1), 178-197.

DuBois, D. L., and Flay, B. R. (2004). The healthy pursuit of self-esteem: comment on and alternative to the Crocker and Park (2004) formulation. *Psychological Bulletin, 130*(3), 415-420.

Dutton, K. A., and Brown, J. D. (1997). Global self-esteem and specific self-views as determinants of people's reactions to success and failure. *Journal of Personality and Social Psychology, 73*(1), 139-148.

Emler, N. (2001). *Self-esteem: the costs and causes of low self-worth.* York: York Publishing Services Limited.

Ewert, A. (1983). *Outdoor adventure and self-concept: a research analysis.* Eugene: University of Oregon, Center of Leisure Studies.

Ewert, A. W. (1989). *Outdoor adventure pursuits: foundations, models, and theories.* Arizona: Publishing Horizons, Inc.

Faria, L. (1996). Marsh's self-description questionnaire III (SDQ III): adaptation study with Portuguese college students. *Social Behaviour and Personality, 24*(4), 343-350.

Fuller, J. A., Stanton, J. M.., Fisher, G. G., Spitzmüller, C., Russell, S. S., and Smith, P. C. (2003). A lengthy look at the daily grind: time series analysis of events, mood, stress, and satisfaction. *Journal of Applied Psychology, 88*(6), 1019- 1033.

Galinsky., A. D., and Ku, G. (2004). The effects of perspective-taking on prejudice: the moderating role of self-evaluation. *Personality and Social Psychology Bulletin, 30*(5), 594-604.

Gecas, V. and Schwalbe, M L. (1983). Beyond the looking glass self: Social structure and efficacy based self-esteem. *Social Psychology Quarterly, 46, 77-88.*

Gerrard, M., Gibbons, F. X., Reis-Bergan, M., and Russell, D. W. (2000). Self-esteem,
self-serving cognitions, and health risk behaviour. *Journal of Personality, 68*(6), 1177-1201.

Gibbons, F. X., Gerrard, M., Vande Lune, L. S., Ashby Wills, T., Brody, G., and Conger, R. D. (2004). Context and cognitions: environmental risk, social influence, and adolescent substance use. *Personality and Social Psychology Bulletin, 30*(8), 1048-1061.

Greenwald, A. G., Bellezza, F. S., and Banaji, M. R. (1988). Is self-esteem a central ingredient of the self-concept? *Personality and Social Psychology Bulletin, 14*(1), 34-45.

Grocott, A. C., and Hunter, J, A. (2009). Increases in global and domain specific self-esteem following a 10-day developmental voyage. *Social Psychology of Education, (12), 453-459.*

Hall, L. A., Kotch, J. B., Browne, D., and Rayens, M. K. (1996). Self-esteem as a mediator of the effects of stressors and social resources on depressive symptoms in postpartum mothers. *Nursing Research, 45*(4), 231-238.

Hall, P. L., and Tarrier, N. (2003). The cognitive-behavioural treatment of low self-esteem in psychotic patients: a pilot study. *Behaviour Research and Therapy, 41*(3), 317-332.

Harter, S. (1990a). Causes, correlates, and the functional role of global self-worth: a lifespan perspective. In R. J. Sternberg, and J. Kolligian (Eds.), *Competence considered* (pp. 67-97). New Haven: Yale University Press.

Harter, S. (1990b). Self and identity development. In S. S. Feldman, and G. R. Elliott (Eds.), *At the threshold: The developing adolescent* (pp. 352-387). Cambridge: Harvard University Press.

Harter (1993). Causes and consequences of low self-esteem in children and adolescents. In R. F. Baumeister (Ed.), *Self-esteem: the puzzle of low self-regard* (pp.87-116). New York: Plenum Press.

Harter, S. (1996). Teacher and classmate influences on scholastic motivation, self-esteem, and level of voice in adolescents. In J. Juvonen, and K. R. Wentzel (Eds.), *Social Motivation Understanding Children's School Adjustment* (pp. 11-42). New York: Cambridge University Press.

Harter, S. (1998). The development of self-representations. In D. William, and N. Eisenberg (Eds.), *Handbook of Child Psychology* (pp. 553-617). Hoboken: John Wiley and Sons, Inc.

Harter, S. (2003). The development of self-representations during childhood and adolescence. In M. R. Leary, and J. P. Tangney (Eds.), *Handbook of self and identity* (pp.610-642). New York: The Guilford Press.

Harter, S., and Marold, D. B. (1994). The directionality of the link between self-esteem and affect: beyond causal modelling. In D. Cicchetti, and S. L. Toth (Eds.).

Disorders and dysfunctions of the self (pp.333-369). New York: University of Rochester Press.

Harter, S., Stocker, C., and Robinson, N. S. (1996). The perceived directionality of the link between approval and self-worth: the liabilities of a looking glass self-orientation among young adolescents. *Journal of Research on Adolescence, 6*(3), 285-308.

Harter, S., and Whitesell, N. R. (2001). On the importance of importance ratings in understanding adolescents' self-esteem: beyond statistical parsimony. In R. J. Riding, and S. G. Rayner (Eds.), *Self Perception* (pp.3-23). Westport: Ablex Publishing.

Harter, S., and Whitesell, N. R. (2003). Beyond the debate: why some adolescents report stable self-worth over time and situation, whereas others report changes in self-worth. *Journal of Personality, 71*(6), 1027-1058.

Harter, S, Whitesell, N. R., and Junkin, L. J. (1998). Similarities and differences in domain-specific and global self-evaluations of learning-disabled, behaviourally disordered, and normally achieving adolescents. *American Educational Research Journal, 35*(4), 653-680.

Hattie, J. A. (1987). Identifying the salient facets of a model of student learning: a synthesis of meta-analyses. *International Journal of Educational Research, 11,* 187-212.

Hattie, J. (1992). *Self-Concept.* New Jersey: Lawrence Erlbaum Associates, Inc.

Hattie, J., Marsh, H. W., Neill, J. T., and Richards, G. E. (1997). Adventure education and outward bound: out-of-class experiences that make a lasting difference. *Review of Educational Research, 67*(1), 43-87.

Hobfoll, S. E., and Leiberman., J. R. (1987). Personality and social resources in immediate and continued stress resistance among women. *Journal of Personality and Social Psychology, 52*(1), 18-26.

Hodson, G., Dovidio, J. F., and Esses, V. M. (2003). Ingroup identification as a moderator of positive-negative asymmetry in social discrimination. *European Journal of Social Psychology, 33,* 215-233.

Hunter, J. A. (1998). Inter-group evaluative bias and self-esteem among Christians. *Current Research in Social Psychology, 3*(7), 74-87.

Hunter, J. A., Banks, M., O'Brien, K., Kafka, S., Hayhurst, J., Jephson, D., Jorgensen, B., and Stringer M. (2011). Intergroup discrimination involving negative outcomes and self-esteem. *Journal of Applied Social Psychology,* 41, 1145-1174.

Hunter, J. A., Boyes, M., Maunsell, S., and O'Hare, D. (2002). *Sail training in the international arena: the value of sail training to young people today.* Final report for phase one of a project commissioned by the International Sail Training Association (ISTA).

Hunter, J. A., Cox, S. L., O'Brien, K., Stringer, M., Boyes, M., Banks, M., Hayhurst, J. G., and Crawford, M. (2005). Threats to group value, domain-specific self-esteem and intergroup discrimination amongst minimal and national groups. *British Journal of Social Psychology, 44*(3), 329-353.

Hunter, J. A., Kafka, S., Hayhurst, G., Clark, H., Dickerson, D., Harold G., Boyes. M., O'Brien, K., and Stringer, M. (2010). Increased self-efficacy following a 10-day developmental voyage. Child and Adolescent Mental Health, 22, 63-65, (2010).

Hunter, J. A., Platow, M. J., Howard, M. L., and Stringer, M. (1996). Social identity and intergroup evaluative bias: realistic categories and domain specific self-esteem in a conflict setting. *European Journal of Social Psychology, 26,*631-647.

Hunter, J. A., Platow, M. J., Bell, L. M., Kypri, K., and Lewis, C. A. (1997). Intergroup bias and self-evaluation: domain-specific self-esteem, threats to

identity and dimensional importance. *British Journal of Social Psychology, 36,* 405-426.
Hylton, N. (2003). Kids *can* do it! In T. Duder, and K. Thompson (Eds.), *Spirit of youth: thirty years of the Spirit of Adventure trust* (pp. 35-39). Auckland: Exisle Publishing Limited.
Jackson, L. D., and Bracken, B. A. (1998). Relationship between students' social status and global and domain-specific self-concepts. *Journal of School Psychology, 36*(2), 233-246.
James, W. (1981). *The Principles of Psychology.* Cambridge: Harvard University Press. (Original published 1890).
Jordan, C. H., Spencer, S. J., and Zanna, M. P. (2005). Types of high self-esteem and prejudice: how implicit self-esteem relates to ethnic discrimination among high explicit self-esteem individuals. *Personality and Social Psychology Bulletin, 31*(5), 693-702.
Joseph, L. M., and Greenberg, M. A. (2001). The effects of a career transition program on reemployment success in laid-off professionals. *Consulting Psychology Journal: Practice and Research, 53*(3), 169-181.
Kaplan, S., and Frey Talbot, J. (1983). Psychological benefits of a wilderness experience. In I. Altman, and J. F. Wohlwill (Eds.), *Human Behavior and Environment Advances in Theory and Research.. Behavior and the Natural Environment* (Vol. 6) (pp.163-203). New York: Plenum Press.
Karatzias, K. G., Power., and Swanson, V. (2001). Predicting use and maintenance of substances in Scottish adolescents. *Journal of Youth and Adolescence, 30*(4), 465-484.
Kelly, F. J., and Baer, D. J. (1969). Jesness inventory and self-concept measures for delinquents before and after participation in outward bound. *Psychological Reports, 25,* 719-724.
Kiernan, G., Gormley, M., and Maclachlan, M. (2004). Outcomes associated with participation in a therapeutic recreation camping programme for children from 15 European countries: data from the 'Barretstown Studies'. *Social Science and Medicine, 59*(5), 903-913.
Klint, K.A. (1999). New directions for inquiry into self-concept and adventure experiences. In J. C. Miles, and S. Priest (Eds.), *Adventure Programming* (pp. 163–168. State College, PA: Venture Publishing.
Knapen, J., Van de Vliet, P., Van Coppenolle, H., David, A., Peuskens, J., Pieters, G., and Knapen, K. (2005). Comparison of changes in physical self-concept, global self-esteem, depression and anxiety following two different psychomotor therapy programs in nonpsychotic psychiatric inpatients. *Psychotherapy and Psychosomatics, 74,* 353-361.

Lau, P. W. C., Lee, A., Ransdell, L., Yu, C. W., and Sung, R. Y. T. (2004). The association between global self-esteem, physical self-concept and actual *vs* ideal body size rating in Chinese primary school children. *International Journal of Obesity, 28,* 314-319.

Lavender, J. (2003). Voyages for disabled trainees. In T. Duder, and K. Thompson (Eds.), *Spirit of youth: thirty years of the Spirit of Adventure trust* (pp. 61-63). Auckland: Exisle Publishing Limited.

Leary, M. R. (1999a). Making sense of self-esteem. *Current Directions in Psychological Science, 8*(1), 32-35.

Leary, M. R. (1999b). The social and psychological importance of self-esteem. In R. M. Kowalski, and M. R. Leary (Eds.), *The social psychology of emotional and behavioural problems: interfaces of social and clinical psychology* (pp. 197-221). Washington DC, US: American Psychological Association.

Leary, M. R. (2003). Interpersonal aspects of optimal self-esteem and the authentic self. *Psychological Inquiry, 14,* 52-54.

Leary, M. R., and Baumeister, R. F. (2000). The nature and function of self-esteem: sociometer theory. In M. P. Zanna (Ed.), *Advances in experimental social psychology* (Vol.32) (pp. 1-62). San Diego, CA, US: Academic Press.

Leary, M. R., and MacDonald, G. (2003). Individual differences in self-esteem: a review and theoretical integration. In M. R. Leary, and J. P. Tangney (Eds.), *Handbook of self and identity* (pp. 401-418). New York, NY, US: Guilford Press.

Leppington, P. (2003). Changing lives. In T. Duder, and K. Thompson (Eds.), *Spirit of youth: thirty years of the Spirit of Adventure trust* (pp. 40-44). Auckland: Exisle Publishing Limited.

Lopez, M. A., and Heffer, R. W. (1998). Self-concept and social competence of university student victims of childhood physical abuse. *Child Abuse and Neglect, 22*(3), 183-195.

Lott, J. (2003). Learning through expertise. In T. Duder, and K. Thompson (Eds.), *Spirit of youth: thirty years of the Spirit of Adventure trust* (pp. 30-34). Auckland: Exisle Publishing Limited.

Luhtanen, R. K., and Crocker, J. (2005). Alcohol use in college students: effects of level of self-esteem, narcissism, and contingencies of self-worth. *Psychology of Addictive Behaviors, 19*(1), 99-103.

Maddux, J. E., and Gosselin, J. T. (2003). Self-efficacy. In M. R. Leary, and J. P. Tangney (Eds.), *Handbook of self and identity* (pp. 218-238). New York, NY, US: The Gilford Press.

Maggi, S. (2001). Italian version of the Self-Description Questionnaire-III. *International Journal of Testing, 1*(3and4), 245-248.

Marsh, H. W. (1987). The big-fish-little-pond effect on academic self-concept. *Journal of Educational Psychology, 79*(3), 280-295.

Marsh, H. W. (1989). Age and sex effects in multiple dimensions of self-concept: preadolescence to early adulthood. *Journal of Educational Psychology, 81*(3), 417-430.

Marsh, H. W., Barnes, J., and Hocevar, D. (1985). Self-other agreement on multidimensional self-concept ratings: factor analysis and multitrait-multimethod analysis. *Journal of Personality and Social Psychology, 49*(5), 1360-1377.

Marsh, H. W., and Byrne, B. M. (1993). Do we see ourselves as others infer: a comparison of self-other agreement on multiple dimensions of self-concept from two continents. *Australian Journal of Psychology, 45*(1), 49-58.

Marsh, H. W., and Hattie, J. (1996). Theoretical perspectives on the structure of self-concept. In B. A. Bracken (Ed.), *Handbook of self-concept: developmental, social, and clinical considerations* (pp. 38-90). New York: John Wiley and Sons, Inc.

Marsh, H. W., and O'Neill, R. (1984). Self description questionnaire III: the construct validity of multidimensional self-concept ratings by late adolescents. *Journal of Educational Measurement, 21*(2), 153-174.

Marsh, H. W., and Peart, N. D. (1988). Competitive and cooperative physical fitness training programs for girls: effects on physical fitness and multidimensional self-concepts. *Journal of Sport and Exercise Psychology, 10*, 390-407.

Marsh, H. W., Relich, J. D., and Smith, I. D. (1983). Self-concept: the construct validity of interpretations based upon the SDQ. *Journal of Personality and Social Psychology, 45*(1), 173-187.

Marsh, H. W., and Richards, G. E. (1988). The Outward Bound Bridging Course for low-achieving high school males: effect on academic achievement and multidimensional self-concepts. *Australian Journal of Psychology, 40*(3), 281-298.

Marsh, H. W., and Richards, G. E. (1990). Self-other agreement and self-other differences on multidimensional self-concept ratings. *Australian Journal of Psychology, 42*(1), 31-45.

Marsh, H. W., Richards, G. E., and Barnes, J. (1986a). Multidimensional self-concepts: a long-term follow-up of the effect of participation in an outward bound program. *Personality and Social Psychology Bulletin, 12*(4), 475-492.

Marsh, H. W., Richards, G. E., and Barnes, J. (1986b). Multidimensional self-concepts: the effect of participation in an outward bound program. *Journal of Personality and Social Psychology, 50*(1), 195-204.

Marsh, H. W., and Shavelson, R. (1985). Self-concept: it's multifaceted, hierarchical structure. *Educational Psychologist, 20*(3), 107-123.

Marsh, H. W., Smith, I. D., Barnes, J., and Butler, S. (1983). Self-concept: reliability, stability, dimensionality, validity, and the measurement of change. *Journal of Educational Psychology, 75*(5), 772-790.

Marx, R. W., and Winne, P. H. (1978). Construct interpretations of three self-concept inventories. *American Educational Research Journal, 15*(1), 99-109.

McGee, R., Williams, S., Howden-Chapman, P., Martin, J., and Kawachi, I. (2006). Participation in clubs and groups from childhood to adolescence and its effects on attachment and self-esteem. *Journal of Adolescence, 29,* 1-17.

McGovern, J. J., Guida, F., and Corey, P. (2002). Improved health and self-esteem among patients with AIDS in a therapeutic community nursing program. *Journal of Substance Abuse Treatment, 23*(4), 437-440.

McLennan, G., Ryan, A., and Spoonley, P. (2000). *Exploring society: sociology for New Zealand students.* Auckland: Pearson Education New Zealand Limited.

Murray, S. L., Rose, P., Bellavia, G. M., Holmes, J. G., Kusche, A. G. (2002). When rejection stings: how self-esteem constrains relationship-enhancement processes. *Journal of Personality and Social Psychology, 83*(3), 556-573.

Neill, J. (1998). What the research really says. Outward Bound Australia. Retrieved December 14, 2005, from http://www.outwardbound .com.au/pages/ao_research_archive.html

Norris, R. M., and Weinman, J. A. (1996). Psychological change following a long sail training voyage. *Personality and Individual Differences, 21,* 189-194.

Pennix, B. W. J. H., van Tilburg, T., Boeke, A. J. P., Deeg, D. J. H., Kriegsman, D. M. W., and van Eijk, J. T. M. (1998). Effects of social support and personal coping resources on depressive symptoms: different for carious chronic diseases? *Health Psychology, 17*(6), 551-558.

Perez, M., Pettit, J. W., David, C. F., Kistner, J. A., and Joiner, T. E Jr. (2001). The interpersonal consequences of inflated self-esteem in an impatient psychiatric youth sample. *Journal of Consulting and Clinical Psychology,* 69(4), 712-716.

Pyszczynski, T., and Cox, C. (2004). Can we really do without self-esteem?: comment on Crocker and Park (2004). *Psychological Bulletin, 130*(3), 425-429.

Rector, N. A., and Roger, D. (1997). The stress buffering effect of self-esteem. *Personality and Individual Difference, 23*(5), 799-808.

Robins, R. W., Tracy, J. L., Trzesniewski, K., Potter, J., and Gosling, S. D. (2001). Personality correlates of self-esteem. *Journal of Research in Personality, 35,*463-482.

Rosenberg, M. (1965). *Society and the adolescent self-image.* Princeton: Princeton University Press.

Rosenberg, M., Schooler, C., Schoenbach, C., and Rosenberg, F. (1995). Global self-esteem and specific self-esteem: different concepts, different outcomes. *American Sociological Review, 60*(1), 141-157.

Rossman, B. B., and Ulehla, Z. J. Psychological reward values associated with wilderness use: a functional-reinforcement approach. *Environment and Behaviour, 9*(1), 41-66.

Rubin, M., and Hewstone, M. (1998). Social identity theory's self-esteem hypothesis: a review and some suggestions for clarification. *Personality and Social Psychology Review, 2*(1), 40-62.

Salmivalli, C. (2001). Feeling good about oneself, being bad to others? Remarks on self-esteem, hostility, and aggressive behaviour. *Aggression and Violent Behaviour, 6*(4), 375-393.

Salmivalli, C., Kaukiainen, A., Kaistaniemi, L., and Lagerspetz, K. M. J. (1999). Self-evaluated self-esteem, peer-evaluated self-esteem, and defensive egotism as predictors of adolescents' participation in bullying situations. *Personality and Social Psychology Bulletin, 25*(10), 1268-1278.

Scheier, L. M., Botvin, G. J., Griffin, K. W., and Diaz, T. (2000). Dynamic growth models of self-esteem and adolescent alcohol use. *Journal of Adolescence, 20*(2), 178-209.

Shavelson, R. J., Hubner, J. J., and Stanton, G. C. (1976). Self-concept: validation of construct interpretations. *Review of Educational Research, 46*(3), 407-441.

Sheldon, K. M. (2004). The benefits of a "sidelong" approach to self-esteem need satisfaction: comment on Crocker and Park (2004). *Psychological Bulletin, 130*(3), 421-424.

Shimizu, M., and Pelham, B. W. (2004). The unconscious cost of good fortune: implicit and explicit self-esteem, positive life events, and health. *Health Psychology, 23*(1), 101-105.

Smith, G. E., Gerrard, M., and Gibbons, F. X. (1997). Self-esteem and the relation between risk behaviour and perceptions of vulnerability to unplanned pregnancy in college women. *Health Psychology, 16*(2). 137-146.

Sondhaus, E. L., Kurtz, R. M., and Strube, M. J. (2001). Body attitude, gender, and self-concept: a 30-year perspective. *Journal of Psychology, 135*(4), 413-430.

Spirit of Adventure Trust. (2005). Retrieved November 24, 2005, from http://www.spiritof adventure.org.nz

Spoonley, P.(1988). *Critical issues in New Zealand society: racism and ethnicity.* Auckland: Oxford University Press.

Swaim, K. F., and Bracken, B. A. (1997). Global and domain-specific self-concepts of a matched sample of adolescent runaways and nonrunaways. *Journal of Clinical Child Psychology, 26*(4), 397-403.

Taubman - Ben-Ari, O. (2000). The effect of reminders of death on reckless driving: a terror management perspective. *Current Directions in Psychological Science, 9*, 196-199.

Tesser, A. (1988). Toward a self-evaluation maintenance model of social behavior. In L. Berkowitz (Ed.), *Advances in experimental psychology* (Vol.21, pp. 181-227). San Diego, CA, US: Academic Press, Inc.

Tomlinson, A. (2003). A new start. In T. Duder, and K. Thompson (Eds.), *Spirit of youth: thirty years of the Spirit of Adventure trust* (pp. 94-95). Auckland: Exisle Publishing Limited.

Top UK baby names 2003. (2003). Retrieved November 24, 2003, from http://www.babycentre.co.uk/pregnancy/naming/topnames2003/

van Boxtel, H. W., Orobio de Castro, B., and Goossens, F. A. (2004). High self-perceived social competence in rejected children is related to frequent fighting. *European Journal of Developmental Psychology, 1*(3), 205-214.

Webster, G. D., and Kirkpatrick, L. A. (2006). Behavioural and self-reported aggression as a function of domain-specific self-esteem. *Aggressive Behaviour, 32,* 17-27.

Welch, A. (2003). Why the voyagers club works. In T. Duder, and K. Thompson (Eds.), *Spirit of youth: thirty years of the Spirit of Adventure trust* (pp. 57-60). Auckland: Exisle Publishing Limited.

Williams, K. D. (2007). Ostracism. *Annual Review of Psychology, 58*, 425-452.

Wood, J. V., Heimpel, S. A., and Michela, J. L. (2003). Savoring versus dampening: self-esteem differences in regulating positive affect. *Journal of Personality and Social Psychology, 85*(3), 566-580.

Wood, J. V., Heimpel, S. A., Newby-Clark, I. R., and Ross, M. (2005). Snatching defeat from the jaws of victory: self-esteem differences in the experience and anticipation of success. *Journal of Personality and Social Psychology, 89*(5), 764-780.

APPENDIX A

The Short Form of the Self-Description Questionnaire III

Use the scale outlined below to describe how you feel right now (even if you have felt differently at other times). Write the number that you feel is most correct (in the space provided).

1=Definitely False	5=More True Than False
2=False	6=Mostly True
3=Mostly False	7=True
4=More False Than True	8=Definitely True

1. I am quite good at mathematics. ___
2. Spiritual/religious beliefs make my life better and me a better person. ___
3. Overall, I don't have much respect for myself. ___
4. I am a very honest person. ___
5. I have lots of friends of the opposite sex. ___
6. I have a poor vocabulary. ___
7. My parents understand me. ___
8. I worry a lot. ___
9. I have trouble with most school subjects. ___
10. I am good at combining ideas in ways that others have not tried. ___
11. I dislike the way I look. ___
12. I make friends easily with members of the same sex. ___
13. I am a good athlete. ___

APPENDIX B

The Behavioural Willingness to Use Drugs and Alcohol Scale
Use the scale outlined below to describe how you feel right now (even if you have felt differently at other times). Write the number that you feel is most correct (in the space provided).

1=Definitely False   5=More True Than False
2=False   6=Mostly True
3=Mostly False   7=True
4=More False Than True   8=Definitely True

Suppose that you were with a group of friends and there were some drugs that you could have if you wanted

1. Would you be willing to take some and use it? ___
2. Would you be willing to use enough to get high? ___

Suppose that you were with a group of friends and there was some alcohol that you could have if you wanted

1. Would you be willing to take some and drink it? ___
2. Would you be willing to get drunk? ___

APPENDIX C

The Behavioural Intention to Use Drugs and Alcohol Scale
Use the scale outlined below to describe how you feel right now (even if you have felt differently at other times). Write the number that you feel is most correct (in the space provided).

1=Definitely False   5=More True Than False
2=False   6=Mostly True
3=Mostly False   7=True
4=More False Than True   8=Definitely True

1. I plan to take drugs in the next year. ___
2. I plan to drink alcohol in the next year. ___

APPENDIX D

The Physical Aggression Scale

Use the scale outlined below to describe how you feel right now (even if you have felt differently at other times). Write the number that you feel is most correct (in the space provided).

1=Extremely Uncharacteristic of Me
2=Somewhat Uncharacteristic of Me
3=Neither Uncharacteristic Nor Characteristic of Me
4=Somewhat Characteristic of Me
5=Extremely Characteristic of Me

1. Once in a while I can't control the urge to strike another person. ___
2. Given enough provocation, I may hit another person. ___
3. If somebody hits me, I hit him or her back. ___
4. I get into fights a little more than the average person does. ___
5. If I have to resort to violence to protect my rights, I will. ___
6. There are people who pushed me so far that we came to blows. ___
7. I can think of no good reason for ever hitting a person. ___
8. I have threatened people I know. ___
9. I have become so mad that I have broken things. ___

APPENDIX E

The Verbal Aggression Scale

Use the scale outlined below to describe how you feel right now (even if you have felt differently at other times). Write the number that you feel is most correct (in the space provided).

1=Extremely Uncharacteristic of Me
2=Somewhat Uncharacteristic of Me
3=Neither Uncharacteristic Nor Characteristic of Me

4=Somewhat Characteristic of Me
5=Extremely Characteristic of Me

1. I tell my friends openly when I disagree with them. ___
2. I often find myself disagreeing with people. ___
3. When people annoy me, I may tell them what I think of them. ___
4. I can't help getting into arguments when people disagree with me. ___
5. My friends say that I'm somewhat argumentative. ___

APPENDIX F

The Zero-Sum Allocation Racial Bias Task

In the next question that follows, we are interested in how different people divide things up. There are no right or wrong answers here so please don't spend too much time thinking about your reply. Just give the answer that feels right to you "right now", even if you have felt differently at other times.

Imagine that you have $10,000 and that you have to divide this between two people. You may give as much or as little to either person, but you cannot give more than $10,000 overall. How much would you give to:

A person whose parents are from the United Kingdom ___
A person whose parents are from Asia ___

APPENDIX G

The Zero-Sum Allocation Gender Bias Task

In the next question that follows, we are interested in how different people divide things up. There are no right or wrong answers here so please don't spend too much time thinking about your reply. Just give the answer that feels right to you "right now" even if you have felt differently at other times. Imagine that you have $10,000 and that you have to divide this between two people, Jack and Emily. You may give as much or as little to either person, but you cannot give more than $10,000 overall. How much would you give to:

Jack ___
Emily ___

In: Evidence-Based Education
Editors: D. Chun-Lok and V. Wang-Yan © 2012 Nova Science Publishers, Inc.
ISBN: 978-1-61324-927-7

Chapter 3

CRITICAL ANALYSIS OF THE POLICIES OF SCHOOL-BASED MANAGEMENT IN HONG KONG

Dennis Chun-Lok Fung and Valerie Wing-Yan Yip
The University of Hong Kong, Hong Kong

INTRODUCTION

Since the establishment of School-based Management (SBM) in Hong Kong in the 1990s, there have been substantial studies indicating that SBM has few, if any, significant benefits for secondary school students (Tse, 2002). This contradicts the SBM consultation paper, which stated that 'there is evidence of powerful links between the capacities that schools acquire with school-based management and learning outcomes for students though this was less the case in the 1980s and early 1990s, when school-based management tended to be a stand-alone initiative.' (Advisory Committee on School-based Management [ACSM], P.5, 2000)

In this article, by examining the implementation of SBM in two secondary schools in Hong Kong, we argue that the establishment of SBM did has made a difference to students' learning outcomes, although the effects related to SBM are usually difficult to measure (Hannaway, 1996). Specifically, we focused our research on the implementation of the 'Personnel Policies' of the SBM in Hong Kong by investigating the *purposes* and *strategies* stated in the consultation document. By doing so, we studied the implication of the direct linkage called *'Curriculum Policies',* which connected the 'Personnel Policies' and the 'Students' Learning Outcomes'. From a practical point of view, curriculum policies have become vital in determining whether the implementation of SBM in Hong Kong has been successful or not.

LITERATURE REVIEW

Within the broad research area of decentralised management in worldwide educational systems, there has been abundant research related to the effectiveness of SBM in student learning outcomes. Amongst the relevant studies, one of the best-known reviews, conducted by Leithwood and Menzies (1998), which synthesised 83 empirical studies, indicated that there were four forms of SBM : i) Administrative Control, ii) Professional Control, iii) Community Control, and iv) Equal Control. While this study successfully categorised these four areas of SBM, it did not find much evidence of the positive effects of SBM on students' learning.

Based on a review of the literature, we noted that Leithwoord and Menzies's (1998) research only considered the relatively short-term effects of SBM on students' learning rather than looking for the normal emergence of its long-term consequences. While the review commenced in 1985, most of the empirical studies were gathered and examined in the early 1990s, which was only a few years after SBM had been implemented in most developed countries. As a result, we argue that the long-term effects on the students' learning outcomes might have been ignored. In addition, the research admitted that 45 out of the 83 studies appeared to be positive in general although some of those were of poor research quality and lacked statistical underpinnings. Furthermore, there was a limitation addressed in the review in that only 11 studies directly reported the students' achievements, which comprised a very low proportion of the samples in the empirical review.

The second study, which was one of the most significant studies, was conducted by Caldwell (2005) and found that SBM had an impact on students' learning achievements especially in developing countries. In particular, the author conducted a pilot study in 79 Indonesian schools and subsequently found dramatic improvements in the students' academic aspects, notably in the rates of attendance and the test results within 12 months. Comparatively speaking, this study seemed to be more comprehensive than that of Leithwood and Menzies (1998). This is not only because of its originality, but also due to its coverage of developing countries in contrast to Leithwood and Menzies's work, which only considered developed nations.

A similar argument concerning the positive effects of SMB on students' learning was echoed by Fullan and Watson (2000). By synthesising the failures of SBM in several Western countries and identifying the essential conditions of SBM, Fullan and Watson found that there were strategic implications for establishing powerful school-based developments, which positively affected students' learning outcomes. This result, in essence, provided conclusive evidence that positive attainments in students' learning could be achieved if successful strategies of SBM were adopted.

With respect to education policies in Hong Kong, there are always many *purposes* for educational reform to take place, although some of them are officially set out in consultation papers, while others remain as underlying assumptions. Concerning the implementation of SBM related to 'Personnel Policies', the purposes stated in the initial consultation paper were relatively vague compare to those in the later SBM documents. Specifically, the main purpose in the initial document was to 'provide freedom for schools to make decisions on the delivery of educational services, and the flexibility to deploy resources in ways which will best meet the particular needs of the students' (ACSM, P.1, 2000). Generally speaking, the document did not substantially address any specific measures which should be implemented when SBM was still in the early stages of the consultation process.

After a few years of consultation and several amendments of the Education Ordinance in Hong Kong in 2004, clearer and more substantial purposes of SBM evolved. In particular, the prime purpose of SBM became to 'devolve the decision on student learning and resource deployment to the school in order to enable the school to meet the needs of students and enhance their outcomes' (Education and Manpower Bureau [EMB], 2006, p.1). The document aimed to enhance the transparency and accountability of school operation and, not surprisingly, it started to focus on the needs of students and stressed the relationship between SBM and students' learning outcomes. According to the document, the implementation of SBM in the aspect of 'Personnel Policies' included the following areas: (EMB, P.5, 2006)

1. 'Schools are given the authority to approve appointment, acting appointment, re-grading and promotion of teachers, employ substitute teachers and approve leave applications etc.'
2. 'The principal is the leader of a school. To enhance the professionalism and competence of school principals, the Government

has developed a principals' continuous professional development framework to ensure the ever-improving capacity of aspiring, newly appointed and serving principals as professionals and competent leaders of schools in facing the challenges of a knowledge-based society.'
3. 'Performance of teachers and principals is a critical factor for quality school education. The government requires all public sector schools to put in place a fair and open appraisal system. The staff appraisal system can serve both the purposes of professional development and accountability as it can provide information on the quality of staff performance and their training needs.'

Apart from the 'officially' written purposes, the 'Personnel Policies' also served certain underlying purposes. Firstly, the authority of schools in approving appointments could greatly reduce the cost of bureaucracy. With repetitive procedures and tedious paper work eliminated, the schools could focus their resources on teaching instead of clerical work. These decentralisation measures facilitated the concept of school-based budgeting (SBB), which shifted decision-making responsibilities from district office to school stakeholder (Hadderman, 1999). This measure was obviously the first hint of the Education and Manpower Bureau (EMB) in Hong Kong, which actively considered providing flexibility to schools by giving a block grant subsidy including teachers' salaries, like the Direct Subsidy Scheme (DSS), after the implementation of SBM. Secondly, this new policy could save a considerable amount of clerical work in the EMB which would mean a dramatic cut of government expenditure. It provided a sound reason for the EMB to shrink its budget especially in 2000, when there was a projected government deficit of $36.5 billion due to the economic downturn. Finally, the establishment of a continuous professional development framework for school principals was considered as a precursor to the later proposal which strongly recommended that in-service teachers be given 150 Continuing Professional Development (CPD) hours each year. Following the above discussion of the purposes of SBM, I shall discuss the SBM *strategies* adopted by different regions before we examine this issue in Hong Kong. In particular, one of the most systematic studies on the strategies of educational decentralisation was conducted by Hanson (1998) which investigated examples from five regions: Colombia, Venezuela, Argentina, Nicaragua and Spain. The study illustrated that different SBM strategies affected the outcomes of the education reforms in these countries. Another study, which was conducted by Fullan and Watson

(1999), reviewed the success and failure of SBM in different Western countries. Specifically, Fullan and Watson found that the most successful strategies of SBM included building relations among teachers inside and outside school, developing a greater degree of cultural shift and redistributing power at the school level. The research indeed paralleled that of Nenyod (2002), who investigated the implementation of SBM in Thailand. In particular, Nenyod indicated that the implementation of SBM through a whole-school approach had led to a positive effect on students' learning. This result was further underpinned by Mohrman (1993), who found that the transition from a traditional management method to an SBM approach was best accompanied by establishing cooperation between different stakeholders in schools. However, the SMB implementation strategy adopted in Hong Kong, whereby a pilot scheme was initially launched before its full establishment, was significantly different to the mandatory constitution of SBM in Western countries. More specifically, the initiatives for the policy to transform all public schools into school-based management institutions can be traced back to 1991, when the Education Department (ED) launched a new scheme called 'School Management Initiative' (SMI). This initiative, which devised a prototype of a school-based management framework for all public schools, was considered as a pilot scheme for the forthcoming SBM policies. With positive responses, the number of schools participating in the SMI had increased from 21 secondary schools in 1992 to 148 in 1997. At the same time, 199 primary and 18 special schools had joined the scheme (Cheng, 2001).

It is the belief of this researcher that the practice of launching a pilot framework of SMI before the formal suggestion by the Education Commission in 2000, which required all Hong Kong public schools to implement SBM, was worthwhile. This is because the SMI scheme successfully attracted a large number of scholars in universities to investigate the process and the impact of its implementation. The advice of these scholars, indeed, contributed a lot towards the evaluation of the SMI scheme. From 1993 to 1997, the Advisory Committee on SMI had set up a task group of evaluation to monitor and evaluate the SMI implementation and its effectiveness. While it seemed that the committee would successfully make this initiative part of a well-constructed SBM framework in 1997, the continuous waves of education reform in Hong Kong during the late 1990s adversely affected the implementation of SBM. Firstly, the announcement of the mandatory implementation of SBM in 1997 severely broke the trust between the School Sponsoring Bodies (SSB) and the government when the negotiation was still ongoing regarding the issue of restructuring school governance. This was indicated by a newspaper article written by Joseph Zen Ze-Kiun, who served as the sixth Bishop of Hong Kong, which stated that 'there is a better way to promote school based management. The new policy will damage the well-established system, bypass the sponsoring bodies and create the danger of politicising school management. We think that the government owes us an explanation of why they are so adamant in imposing this uniform model.' (Zen, 2004). Secondly, the first Chief Executive of Hong Kong, Mr. Tung Chee-hwa, presented his important blueprint for education reform for the new century, which incorporated SBM as one of the major reforms. In essence, the high profile of the 'unfavourable' reform policies associated with the comprehensive review of school curriculum, promotion of IT education, introduction of the mandatory scheme for the medium of instruction and the establishment of benchmarks for English teachers seriously undermined the potential of SBM in obtaining support from the teachers and stakeholders. Finally, SBM in Hong Kong was arguably imported from Western countries directly without a thorough discussion about the capacity of teachers who should play a key role in facilitating the relevant policies (Wan, 2005). The implementation of SBM confused the traditional role of the teacher, who was solely responsible for teaching rather than being accountable for policy implementation. Concerning the aim of SBM to provide schools with the authority to approve staff appointments, promotion and leave applications, it seemed that there was no specific strategy to promote this new personnel policy. However, a higher degree of flexibility was given to schools with regard to IT funding, the Quality Education Fund (QEF) and other block grant funding. On the other hand, the Education Department set up a task group in 1999 to train aspiring and in-service principals by providing an educational leadership programme. This aligned with the SBM personnel policy which aimed to provide continuous professional development to school principals. In order to ensure that schools followed the SBM personnel policy in setting up a fair and open appraisal system, the Education Department required all schools to conduct a self-evaluation each year which would subsequently be reviewed by the External School Review (ESR).

METHODOLOGY

Based on the aspect of 'Personnel Policies', we conducted a small-scale study on the implementation of these policies in two secondary schools in Hong Kong. Specifically, both schools had fully implemented SBM in the years 1992 and 2000 respectively. The first school (School A), which was situated on the Kowloon peninsula, was recognised informally as a pioneering school in adopting SBM since it was one of the pilot schools that had implemented SBM in 1992. The second school (School B), which had been built during the 1990s, was situated on Hong Kong Island and had implemented the SBM several years after its founding. The principal of School A was very experienced and had been head of the school for more than 25 years. His leadership style was recognised as 'principal-centred' or 'administrative control' concerning the implementation of SBM. On the other hand, the leadership mode of the young principal in School B seemed to be 'teacher-centred' or 'professional control'. Both schools had a similar intake and enrolment of over 1000 students. The class structure and staff establishment were almost the same. We adopted a mixed methods approach in this research. In both schools, a questionnaire-based survey was conducted among 30 students, three of whom were invited to join the follow-up in-depth interviews. Similarly, we collected questionnaires from three teachers in each school who taught English, Physics and Mathematics. After we screened through the questionnaires, we decided to interview the English teachers in both schools. Other than the data collected from questionnaire and in-depth interviews, we obtained the students' academic scores in the HKCEE from the participant teachers and the school websites.

RESULT AND DATA ANALYSIS

Based on the curriculum policies of SBM, we designed a questionnaire to collect the students' and teachers' opinions about their school curriculum. This research successfully gathered 30 questionnaires from School A and B respectively and no missing data were collected. The result was a good indicator of whether the implementation of SBM in the curriculum design affected students' learning outcomes. According to the results shown in table 1, a large proportion of students expressed that their schools had already implemented SBM. This might have been due to the publicity conducted by EMB and the newspaper coverage of the issue related to the restructuring of school governance raised by Bishop Zen. Numerically speaking, more than half and about 30% of students in School A and School B respectively agreed that their schools provided essential learning experience, a happy and open learning environment, proper supportive measures and a student-centred teaching method.

Table 1. Students' responses in questionnaire-based survey

Question (%)	Strongly Disagree	Disagree	Neutral	Agree	Strongly Agree	School
1. I am aware that my school has implemented the Curriculum Policies of SBM	13				87	A
	17				83	B
I am aware that my school provides its own diversified, balanced, flexible and coherent school-based curriculum in line with the objectives of education in HK.	17	33	7	43	0	A
	43	27	7	23	0	B
I am aware that my school provides students with essential learning experiences, and a happy and open learning environment.	7	17	17	33	27	A
	17	7	47	17	13	B
I am aware that my school provides proper support measures and diversified learning activities to ensure the all-round and healthy development of students.	0	10	30	40	20	A
	7	13	50	17	13	B
I am aware that teaching in my school is student-centered, with clear objectives to help students construct knowledge, stimulate thinking, learn how to learn and develop positive attitudes and values.	0	10	23	33	33	A
	7	20	43	30	0	B
I am aware that my school has designed a clear assessment policy to reflect the performance of students.	10	23	17	33	17	A
	20	30	23	17	10	B

The result of students' questionnaires

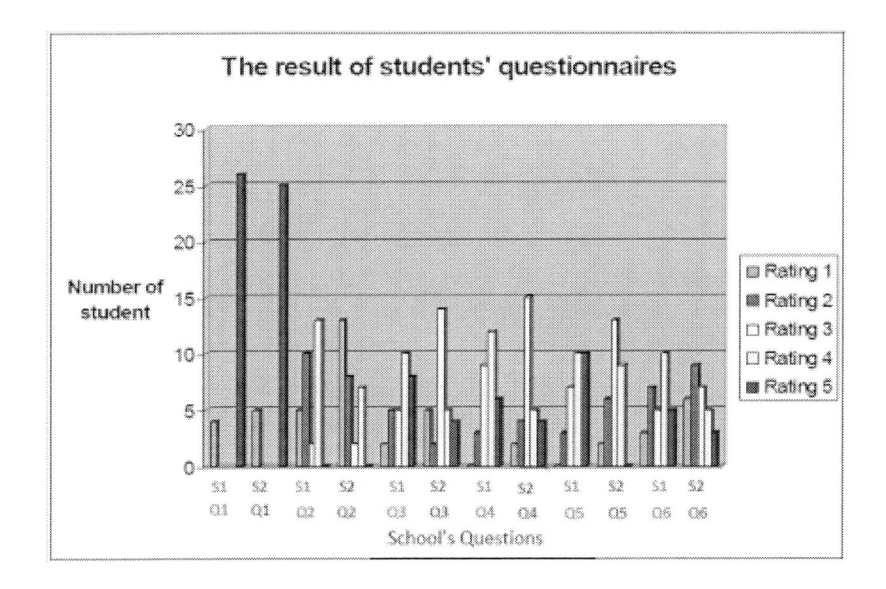

Figure 1. Comparison of students' responses in School A (S1) and School B (S2).

However, there were relatively disappointing results in the aspect of the schools providing a diversified curriculum and clear assessment policy to reflect the performance of students. About one-third to around half of the students in School A and School B showed their disagreement in the corresponding question items. In general, the results indicating the failure of the schools to provide a diversified curriculum could be more or less explained by the existence of the examination-oriented system in Hong Kong. Concerning the two participating schools, it was obvious that the curriculum policies in School A were more effective than in School B for all questions (See figure 1). Based on the information gathered, this might be due to the fact that School A had implemented SBM far longer than School B, for 8 years, and because of the difference in leadership style between the two principals. In the teacher questionnaire, there were eight questions: i) I am aware that HK schools should implement SBM, ii) I am aware that HK schools have been given the authority to approve appointments, and acting appointments, iii) I am aware that HK schools have been given the authority to approve re-grading and promotion of teachers, iv) I am aware that HK schools have been given the authority to employ substitute teachers and approve leave applications, v) I am aware that in HK, the principal is the leader of a school, vi) I am aware that the government has developed a principals' continuous professional development framework, vii) I am aware that HK schools should establish a fair and open appraisal system, and viii) I am aware that the appraisal system serves the purposes of both professional development and accountability. Concerning the teachers' responses, the results showed coherence between the teachers' awareness of personnel policies in SBM in Hong Kong and their own schools' personnel policies. They indicated that both schools strictly followed the SBM policies which were promoted by the government. However, most teachers expressed conservative views towards the school's authority to approve staff leave applications and to set up a fair appraisal system. These disappointing results revealed that the transparency of the two schools' appraisal systems was still very low after the schools had already been implementing the SBM personnel policies for several years. Furthermore, the teachers' responses to the second and the third sets of questions (See appendix 1) showed that there was a disconnection between the teachers' recognition of their schools' personnel policies and the schools' curriculum policies. They reflected that although the SBM personnel policies worked properly in school, the policies had no significant effect on the school curriculum. It might be a catastrophe for the implementation of SBM implementation since SBM aimed to have a positive influence on the school curriculum and the students' learning outcomes. Nevertheless, despite the disconnection between the teachers' recognitions of personnel policies and curriculum policies, the comparatively high rate of students' agreement concerning the positive effects on their learning outcomes could not be denied. The positive effect of SBM on the students' learning outcomes was also indicated by the improvement in their HKCEE results after a certain period of implementation (See figure 2). In this study, the 'success' of the implementation of SBM policies included the successful implementation of SBM at the school's senior management level, the recognition from teachers and, most importantly, the positive effects of SBM on students' learning outcomes.

	Hong Kong Certificate of Education Examination (HKCEE) Overall subjects Passing Rate											
Year	1992	1993	1994	1995	1996	1997	1998	1999	2000	2001	2002	2003
School A	82.3%	85.6%	92.3%	90.6%	92.5%	90.3%	93.6%	90.6%	92.6%	93.5%	92.5%	93.5%
School B	----	-----	----	----	----	----	----	----	72.3%	78.2%	80.3%	93.2%

Figure 2. HKCEE results of School A and School B.

On the other hand, 'failure' simply referred to a failure to achieve the above purposes. In order to investigate the effectiveness of SBM policies at the school management level, we interviewed two English subject panel chairpersons from School A and School B. An extract is given below:

Author1: How do you understand the implementation of SBM policies in your school?
Teacher1: In general, I think that it is a sort of writing many annual reports etc.
Author:1 How about the new policy of the school in appointing teachers and setting up appraisal system?
Teacher1: I think that it has provided flexibility for the school. For example, we had several colleagues who requested study leave in order to attend an English immersion course last year. The principal was given authority by SBM to hire supply teachers.
Author: 1 How about the appraisal system? Is it fair and open?
Teacher2: Frankly, it is always subjective to assess a teacher's performance. However, under the SBM framework, the appraisal system has become more systematic. Each teacher will be assessed by the principal at the end of an academic year. The criteria and procedures have become more open.

We have no doubt that the SBM policies that provided the schools with the authority to appoint teachers have gained support from senior teachers and principals. This is because the policies have benefited schools by offering them a higher degree of autonomy in teacher deployment. This result was verified by the quantitative data obtained from the teacher questionnaires.

However, one teacher gave his opinion in the questionnaire as: 'I think that my school has established a fair and open appraisal system, but I haven't noticed any effects on the promotion and demotion systems. Basically, promotion still strongly depends on the subjective view of principal, not the result of appraisal.'

In addition, another teacher also expressed his view of SBM in the questionnaire: 'SBM is not a good idea for me since I need to do more paper work, even though it may be good for the school. However, by keeping myself more positive, I always remind myself that drafting the annual report can give me new insights for next year'.

DISCUSSION

In this study, an investigation into the implementation of SBM related to the personal policies in two secondary schools in Hong Kong identified the positive effects on students' learning outcomes. While conclusive evidence was obtained from the in-depth interviews and the questionnaire-based surveys, the data of the public examination provided a triangulation of the results.

According to the quantitative and qualitative results, teachers recognised the value of the implementation of SBM in their schools. The high rate of agreement in the questionnaire items related to their schools' personnel policies reflected their general acceptance of SBM. Nevertheless, based on the results of the teacher questionnaire, this was not the case for curriculum policies. Therefore, there was a phenomenon that the phase of curriculum reform lagged behind the phase of personnel policies reform. To a certain extent, this adversely affected the potential for greater improvement in students' learning. As a result, we suggest that the government should conduct an all-round evaluation of the curriculum policies in SBM. Supportive measures should be provided to the middle level managers of schools, which were also supported by Yu (2005).

LIMITATION

The major limitation of this study was the small number of respondents: only six teachers and sixty students participated in the project. Moreover, as we only invited secondary four students to participate in my research, the diversity of the students' participation was limited.

APPENDIX 1

Teacher's recognition of their school SBM for Personnel Policies

Question
I recognise that my school has implemented SBM
I recognise that my school was given the authority to approve appointment and acting appointments
I recognise that my school was given the authority to approve re-grading and promotion of teachers

Question
I recognise that my school was given the authority to employ substitute teachers and approve leave applications.
I recognise that the principal is the leader of my school.
I recognise that my school is transparent to the public
I recognise that my school has established a fair and open appraisal system.
I feel that the appraisal system serves the propose of professional development in my school
I feel that the appraisal system serves the propose of accountability in my school

Teacher's recognition of own school SBM for Curriculum Policies

Question
I recognise that my school has implemented the curriculum policies of SBM
I recognise that my school provides its own diversified, balanced, flexible and coherent school-based curriculum in line with the objectives of education in Hong Kong.
I recognise that my school provides students with essential learning experiences, a happy and open learning environment.
I recognise that my school provides proper support measures and diversified learning activities to ensure all-round and healthy development of students.
I recognise that teaching in my school is student-centered, with clear objectives to help students construct knowledge, stimulate thinking, learn how to learn and develop positive attitudes and values.
I recognise that my school has designed a clear assessment policy to reflect performance of student.

REFERENCES

Advisory Committee on School-based Management. (2000). Transforming Schools into Dynamic and Accountable Professional Learning Communities: School-based Management Consultation Document. Hong Kong: The Government Printer.

Caldwell, B. J., P. International Institute for Educational and E. International Academy of (2005). School-based management, International Institute for Educational Planning (IIEP) Brussels: International Academy of Education (IAE), Paris.

Cheng, Y. C. (2001). Education reforms in Hong Kong: Challenges, strategies, and international implications.

Education and Manpower Bureau. (2006). What is School-based Management. Hong Kong: The Government Printer.

Fullan, M. and N. Watson (2000). "School-based management: Reconceptualizing to improve learning outcomes." SCHOOL EFFECTIVENESS AND SCHOOL IMPROVEMENT-LISSE- 11(4): 453-474.

Hannaway, J. (1996). "Management descentralization and performance based incentives: theoretical consideration for schools." *Improving America's schools. The role of incentives.*

Hanson, E. M. (1998). "Strategies of educational decentralization: key questions and core issues." *Journal of Educational Administration* 36(2): 111-128.

Leithwood, K. and T. Menzies (1998). *"Forms and effects of school-based management: A review." Educational policy* 12(3): 325.

Mohrman, S. A. (1994). *School-Based Management: Organizing for High Performance,* Jossey-Bass Inc., Publishers, 350 Sansome Street, San Francisco, CA 94104.

Nenyod, B. "School-Based Management: Thai Ways and Methods*.".*" *Report to ONEC and ADB as part of TA.*

Tse, K. C. (2002). *"A critical review of the quality education movement in Hong Kong."* Globalization and Education: the quest for quality education in Hong Kong: 143–170.

Wan, E. (2005). *"Teacher empowerment: Concepts, strategies, and implications for schools in Hong Kong."* The Teachers College Record 107(4): 842-861.

Yu, H. (2005). "Implementation of school-based management in Hong Kong: Recent development and future challenges." *Journal of Educational Change* 6(3): 253-275.

Zen Ze-Kiun. (2004). Sharing Session for Principals, Parents, Teachers and Alumni of Catholic Schools. Bishop Zen's Remarks. (9-2-2004) http://www.catholic.org.hk/zen_edu/e040209.html

In: Evidence-Based Education
Editors: D. Chun-Lok and V. Wang-Yan © 2012 Nova Science Publishers, Inc.
ISBN: 978-1-61324-927-7

Chapter 4

PARENTAL INVOLVEMENT IN CHILDREN'S READING: A CULTURAL PERSPECTIVE

Valerie W. Y. Yip and Dennis C. L. Fung
The University of Hong Kong, Hong Kong

ABSTRACT

This study aimed to understand how socially deprived parents in a Chinese society supported their children's reading at home. By examining the interview data gathered from questionnaires and interviews completed by the parents of second grade students, they were found to be supportive to reading with their children and to preparing a suitable environment for learning to read. Although the caregivers had a restricted understanding of their roles and of parent-child reading techniques, they nonetheless believed in their own capabilities. If they encountered difficulties, the families also tried to make use of their local networks. The parents transformed these beliefs into action in response to their role awareness and expectations of their children's future. Such beliefs and behaviours were strongly associated with their commitment to Chinese culture.

INTRODUCTION

Research over the years has confirmed the socio-economic status of a family exerts strong influence on individual's success in schooling. For instance, a meta-analysis points out that home difference could affect children's readiness to benefit from schooling, especially at the primary school level (Kellagan, 1994). Another study, the National Child Development Survey (NCDS) carried out for a cohort of British people born in a week of 1958, disadvantaged children were six times as likely to be poor readers at the age of seven, and fifteen times as likely to be non-readers (Davie, Butler and Goldstein, 1972). Working class children usually had a deficient language environment at home, and consequently they had weaker language skills and poorer performance at school (Tizard and Hughes, 2002, p.109).

It is not surprising that socially disadvantaged families usually participate less at home than their rich counterparts (Ho, 2003). A lot of researchers try to find a causal link between heightened parental involvement and improvement in children's learning. However, it is argued that an understanding of *how* parents engage in children's education is necessary before concluding that parental involvement can improve their school performance. As pointed out by Pomerantz and her colleagues (Pomerantz, Moorman, and Litwack, 2007), more parental involvement may not necessarily lead to better children's learning. Rather, answers on how they get involved can explain why their participation can fulfill the promises.

In a similar vein, there has been voluminous research studying whether parent-child reading can influence children's reading performance and most of the results are positive (Tizard, Schofield and Hewison, 1982; Hannon, 1987; Loveday and Simmons, 1988; Kirby, 1992; Stuart, Dixon, Masterson and Quinlan, 1998; Sénéchal and LeFevre, 2002). Nevertheless, the available evidences still generate a lot of uncertainties about the causal link between parental involvement in reading and reading performance. Then what actually affect children's reading at home? Has there been anything missed out in the previous studies? As pointed out by Hannon (1987), student achievement in reading might only reflect part of the story. An understanding of the interaction between children and parents is necessary before any evaluation can be carried out. Furthermore, more comprehensive measures to reveal parent-child reading at home have to be developed before attempting to establish such link (Dearing, McCartney, Weiss, Kreider, and Simplins, 2004).

Parent-Child Reading in a Chinese Society (Hong Kong)

Parent reading has been a key task of curriculum reform in Hong Kong since the millennium. The Education Bureau (the former Education and

Manpower Bureau before 2007) has made appeal to gain parental support in reading with children[1,2]. Although a lot of resources have been put forward for schools to get them engaged, there has not been any empirical study to provide a comprehensive review of parent-child reading at home. In other words, the government just holds an assumption that the caregivers will give more support to their children in reading with its promotion and good-will. On the other hand, the latest results of PISA (Programme for International Student Assessment) 2009 indicates that Hong Kong 15-year-old students ranked fourth among the participants of 65 countries and regions (CHUK, 2010). We envisage such student achievement should not be the effort of the government and schools alone. Parental involvement in reading at an early stage should be a crucial factor to establish this success.

This study aims to understand how socially deprived parents of second grade students in a Chinese society (Hong Kong) supported their children's reading at home. Our research questions are:

- How did parents get involved in reading with children at home and preparing a reading environment?
- Why did they get engaged in parent-child reading?
- Did socio-economic background affect their participation? What other factor(s) influenced their practices?

METHODOLOGY

There are two main sources of evidence in this study: parents' questionnaire and interviews. The parent participants came from four primary schools purposely selected for their locations in socially deprived regions of Hong Kong. 209 parents completed the questionnaire to report on their background and their beliefs in reading with their children. These 209 families

---

[1] Letter from the Permanent Secretary for Education and Manpower Bureau on "Promotion of Reading Culture in School". Hong Kong: Education and Manpower Bureau, Sept 2002. Accessed from the World Wide Web at http://www.emb.gov.hk/FileManager/TC/Content_3990/e.pdf on 1st June 2006.

[2] Speech of the Permanent Secretary for Education and Manpower Bureau on the Conference 「學會閱讀：世界各地的先進經驗和香港小學生的表現」 (24/5/2003). Accessed from the World Wide Web at http://www.emb.gov.hk/FileManager/TC/Content_ 3990/psemspeech 0503.pdf on 1st June 2006.

were generally socially disadvantaged. More than half received various types of social assistance and lived in public housing. Thirty-seven per cent of families had new immigrant members, among which more than 70 per cent were the parent themselves. There were a few single-parent families. On the other hand, many parents had basic education up to Secondary 3. Cantonese, a local dialect used in Hong Kong, remained as the major language used at home.

Of the 209 parents, thirty-two shared their experience of parent-child reading in the interviews. They had similar family profiles as the survey respondents. About 60 per cent received various types of allowances such as travel and textbook assistances. Fourteen per cent of the families received Comprehensive Social Security Assistance, which requires an annual assessment on family income by the Social Welfare. Sixty per cent lived in public housing estates or temporarily housing, whereas only half of them received basic education up to Secondary 3.

FINDINGS AND DISCUSSIONS

Parent-Child Reading at Home

Most of the parent interviewees claimed that they read with their children in the previous six months. Eighty-seven per cent of them told stories, read aloud, read together with their children or asked the students to read aloud. A parent said:

> "I tell stories after she finishes her homework. We read at least five times each week."

Despite many interviewees claimed to read with their children, only 19 per cent had a fixed schedule. The information was consistent with, but not higher than, the finding of a local online survey[3]. The caregivers usually carried out the practice when both parties were free. Some parents made it before bed; some read after finishing homework and others took reading as a leisure activity. A few families only read once per fortnight. The duration of reading

---

[3] Parent-Child Reading Survey in Hong Kong Families 《香港家庭親子閱讀習慣調查》 was conducted online from April to May 2003. It successfully interviewed 1,141 parents and the statistics was given in Appendix 15. Retrieved from World Wide Web at http://www.rthk.org.hk/press/chi/20030509_66_78201.html on 31st October 2010.

also varied from five minutes to about 30 minutes each time. As told by a parent:

> "I cannot read with my son for a long time. It is usually about 15 minutes. Moreover, he cannot keep quiet all the time."

The lack of a regular schedule and a fixed duration reflects a majority of parents and children were very busy in Hong Kong. After a whole-day school, homework supervision, revision and having adequate rest had higher priority over reading. Moreover, reading was treated as tool for academic excellence or literacy development, as reflected by the parents' beliefs to be discussed in a later section. Unless the parents had a strong belief in the benefits of reading, it was less likely for them to keep up with the schedule. On the other hand, the second graders were still young. Their concentration span was not long enough to read more than 30 minutes unless the parents were skillful enough to retain their attention.

For the families which practised parent-child reading, it could be traced back to the infant level. Two out of the 32 interviewees started to read simple prints with their children when they were about several months old. Forty-four per cent had made it since kindergarten and the remaining continued the practice though they could not remember the exact starting time. As the children got older, parents intended to reduce the frequency. An Everson parent said:

> "I seldom make it now. It was feasible when he was in kindergarten."

The possible reasons of the dropping frequency included parents' time, time constraint of a whole-day school, better language proficiency of children and an urge of being independent (requested by the students, parents or both). It seemed that a drop in frequency, a lack of schedule and a fixed duration were common. Although the frequency did not decrease for some families, they changed the format of reading. A parent reduced the exaggeration used in storytelling, while the others guided the children to read first and asked questions to test their comprehension and understanding.

> "When my daughter was still in the kindergarten, she did not know so many words. Now she is capable to read more. Therefore I ask questions and she answers."

Concerning the mode of parent-child reading, storytelling was the most popular method. Fifty-three per cent of interviewees had the experience to tell stories. Children's literature usually had a lot of illustrations. They did not only attract students' attention, but also helped them to understand the texts especially when they lack the vocabulary and comprehension. The variety of content and hidden messages provided a lot of opportunities to think beyond the contexts. The interviewees also found it easier to tell stories rather than to read non-fictions. There was a space for them to figure out how to present the story in a lively way.

Other than storytelling, 28 per cent of parents asked the students to read aloud for diagnosing the words they did not know. It was also useful to learn a new language and train communication skills.

> "I let him read aloud because it makes him speak. He can become more confident."

Parent-child interaction was another objective of teaching the children to read. As reported by half of the interviewees, the commonest type of interaction was answering the students' enquiries. For example,

> "My son starts to question before I share the book with him! For instance, he asked 'how could the dinosaurs fly?' I told him there were many types of dinosaurs. Then he asked about the classification of different dinosaurs."

The questioning process was not one-way. Forty-four per cent of caregivers also asked questions to ensure their children were attentive and understand the information of the article.

> "I found it is alright to ask her questions when I tell the stories. She understands the things I have talked about."

Having a favourable environment at home is important for the development of reading interests and habits. This includes implementing reading schedules, preparing reading materials for the children by book purchase, library visits and/or book loan, as well as imposing regulations to foster reading.

Sixty-nine per cent of interviewees purchased books and 25 per cent bought children's magazines. Parents usually considered three factors before making the decision: whether the students were interested in the articles, whether the content was educational and the family conditions. Moreover, most parent interviewees preferred using Chinese articles for the sake of children's language proficiency. A parent especially pointed out the native language should be learnt properly. English was more 'distant' from the children. A few families purposely chose English materials. This indicates parents had a basic understanding of selecting the materials. When it came to book selection, 59 per cent of interviewees tried to support the selection process. They reviewed similar strategies, for instance, screening the books for the children (19%), giving freedom for them to choose (22%), or using both methods (41%). Parents wished their children would enjoy reading if they were allowed to select themselves. At the same time, parents' choices could ensure the reading materials were appropriate to promote literacy and learning. The parents also tried to make a balance between the length of texts and the amount of pictures for achieving different purposes.

"I use books with fewer texts and more pictures for storytelling."

Nevertheless, some parents, especially the less educated and less confident, could face difficulties to screen the books for their children. In this case, they either relied on external support or adopted a 'let-go' approach.

"My daughter selects the books she is interested in. I don't know how to make it." (a parent who was educated in Mainland China up to F.3)

The approaches of screening the materials were also related to whether they would be bought or borrowed. Families, irrespective of their socioeconomic status, did not mind to purchase the reading materials. However, most interviewees considered many factors before they made the decisions. Both book purchase and book loan have their pros and cons. For book purchase, it could be quite expensive since each cost more than HK$30 (US$4). Two parents preferred to spend the money on buying academic books like exercises instead. Space at home was another concern. On the average, each person could only have 12.6m^2 of living space in the public housing of Hong Kong[4]. The congested living environment was a factor considered by most interviewees.

---

[4]Statistical data from the Hong Kong Housing in Figures (2010), available from the Hong Kong Housing Authority website http://www.housingauthority.gov.hk/hdw/content/document/ en/aboutus/resources/statistics/HIF2010.pdf accessed on 30th November 2010.

> "I think it is related to the space at home. Our apartment is small, you know. Hong Kong is a small place. We have already filled the upper part of the bunk bed with books."

In addition, the interviewees always complained about their children did not repeat reading the articles they had at home. They even put down the books without having in-depth reading. When the students grew older, their preferences changed. Book purchase could be more economic unless there were more siblings in a family.

> "When my daughters go to bookstores, they can buy one or two they loved most…The books should have good quality so that my girls can share and donate to others when they finish reading them. Our third consideration is whether they are available in the library."

Consequently, the number of interviewees who preferred to borrow books was the same as those who supported book purchase. Although parents sometimes disliked the availability of reading materials on loan, the book conditions ('old' or 'torn') and the environment of the public libraries ('small', 'smelly', 'chaotic' or 'noisy'), 66 per cent still brought their children to the public libraries or borrowed books for them without the presence of the students. A few families visited the bookstores but did not make any purchase. This is consistent with the observation of Coleman (1994). Although disadvantaged parents did not possess the economic and cultural goods, they still made use of the social resources flexibly to build favourable reading environment at home.

On the other hand, the frequency of library visits varied a lot among families. Only 22 per cent had a fixed schedule. Some visited once per fortnight while the others could only make it occasionally. The proximity of public libraries also affected the families in making regular visits. In some areas without stationary libraries, the government sends mobile ones at a weekly basis. An interviewee reflected she liked the mobile library, while two rarely utilized the service as it was too small to stay long enough for selecting books. It was hard to keep their children in a lorry. In this case, poor families might rely more on school to provide the reading materials for reading at home.

Having a stock of reading materials was also common in Hong Kong families. Fifty-six per cent of interviewees had at least a few children books at home. These materials could be accumulated for a child over the years, shared between several children in the family or donated by the relatives.

Unfortunately book recycling might not benefit the children a lot since they might not suit their level.

> "Her auntie gave many books to my daughter when her children grew up; however, she doesn't read. Our educational level is lower than her auntie. Some books are in English which cannot be easily understood. Moreover, the texts are long and the pictures are far away from the texts. My girl may not like this."

Imposing family rules was another dimension of preparing a reading environment. Twenty-five per cent of interviewees restricted their children from watching television or playing with computer. This allowed the parents to suggest the students to read at leisure times and turn it into a habit.

> "My twin daughters read for leisure as they don't have much entertainment. If they don't read, they can just go to the playground for sports activities."

In conclusion, the parents were eager to prepare a reading environment at home. They basically understood how to select the reading materials according to the students' capabilities and interests. They gave freedom for them to choose while they monitored the selection process. Most families were willing to buy books as far as they could afford.

On the other hand, the caregivers also considered book loan for the sake of family finance, space at home and a change in children's preferences. Although the schedule could be irregular, library and bookstore visits were common in the families. Making use of the social resources was a way for them to instill the values of reading into the children.

Parents' Beliefs about Helping Their Children to Read

Previous research has suggested that parents decide how to get involved according to their self-confidence and their perceived roles (Hoover-Dempsey, Walker, Sandler, Whetsel, Green, Wilkens, and Closson, 2005; Nutbrown, Hannon, and Morgan, 2005).

Therefore ten questions were designed to examine their motivational beliefs about helping the students to read. In questions 1 to 7, the caregivers had to indicate whether they were confident to carry out practices such as reading with the children regularly. Their role concepts were explored by questions 8 and 9, which aimed to understand if they believed they were important to children's reading. The following table displays their responses.

Table 1. Parents' motivational beliefs about reading

Question		Mean	Standard deviation	Strongly agree %	Agree %	Not sure %	Disagree %	Strongly disagree %
(1)#	I can read with my child regularly	3.7	.8	10.1	56.7	23.1	10.1	0
(2)#	I can spend at least 10 minutes per week to read with my child	3.9	.8	15.9	66.2	10.6	6.3	1.0
(3)#	I can prepare reading materials for my child	3.8	.8	12.8	59.2	19.9	7.1	.9
(4)#	I can let my child choose their favourite reading materials	4.0	.7	18.6	70.0	7.1	4.3	0
(5)*	I can interact with my child when we read	3.8	.8	12.9	63.2	14.8	8.6	.5
(6)*	I can help to solve his/her reading difficulties	4.0	.6	18.1	71.4	6.2	4.3	0
(7)*	I can recognize my child's needs in reading development	3.6	.8	8.1	58.4	21.1	12.0	.5
(8)@	I play a role to cultivate my child's reading habit	3.7	.9	12.5	58.2	18.3	9.6	1.4
(9)@	I can be his/her role model in reading	3.4	1.0	7.1	47.1	25.2	17.6	2.9

N.B. (1)* = assisting in reading processes; # = preparing a reading environment; @ = role modeling.

(2) 5= strongly agree; 4= agree; 3=not sure; 2=disagree; 1= strongly disagree.

The participating parents generally held positive beliefs in their capabilities to read with their children since more than 60 per cent 'agreed' or 'strongly agreed' with the statements of questions 1 to 8. Caregivers were generally confident to prepare a reading environment at home, for instance, 72 per cent 'strongly agreed' or 'agreed' that they could prepare reading materials for the students (question 3). However, nearly 20 per cent were uncertain about their capabilities. This could partly account for why more parents felt they could give freedom for students to choose their favourite reading materials (89% in question 4). Moreover, maintaining a regular schedule for parent-child reading seemed to be more difficult than having a fixed duration. Sixty-seven per cent 'strongly agreed' or 'agreed' that they could read regularly with the children (question 1), while 82 per cent believed it was possible to spend at least 10 minutes each week to help (question 2). The parents were less certain about the regularity than the length of time they could afford (23% in question 1 compared with 11% in question 2). This implied that parents were willing to spend the time only if their family members had the opportunity to read together.

Other than being confident in preparing a reading environment at home, the parents were positive in the processes of teaching students to read. They especially believed that they could help the students for reading difficulties (90 per cent in question 6) and interact with children (86% in question 5). However, they might be weaker in diagnosing the children's needs of reading development for 21 per cent were uncertain about their capabilities (question 7). Furthermore, parents did not have a clear understanding about their roles in children's reading. Although 71 per cent thought they could play a role to cultivate children's reading habits, 18 per cent were not so sure (question 8). In question 9, 25 per cent were uncertain about their own capacities to be role models. A total of 20 per cent even disagreed with the statement. The possible reasons could be 'role' was quite abstract to some parents and the questionnaire did not provide a definition. Respondents could hold different concepts of parents' roles and role modelling. To some caregivers, performing parents' roles could be simply answering students' questions; while the others could set higher expectations on the regularity and duration of parent-child reading. Their varied depth of understanding about reading influenced their role concepts and role modelling behaviour.

In order to summarize the parents' motivational beliefs, the responses of the ten questions were grouped under the five categories as shown in the footnote of table 1. Questions 5, 6 and 7 were labelled as 'assisting in the reading processes' since they examined the ways parents interacted with the

Table 2. A summary of parents' motivational beliefs

Question	Type of questions	Mean	Standard deviation (SD)
1,2	Preparing reading schedule	3.8	.7
3,4	Preparing reading materials	3.9	.6
5-7	Assisting in reading processes	3.9	.6
8,9	Role modelling of parents	3.6	.8
10	Role of school	3.0	1.3

children during reading. A new mean and new standard deviation (SD) could be given by averaging the respective values of the three items.

Moreover, parents' beliefs about preparing a reading environment at home were examined by either setting a schedule to read regularly and frequently (questions 1 and 2) or providing materials (questions 3 and 4). Another two mean values and two SD could be obtained for these areas. Then questions 8 and 9 were grouped together to form 'role modelling of parents' and gave another mean and SD. Table 2 shows the new average values and standard deviations for the parents' motivational beliefs.

In summary, the parents were confident in their capabilities to prepare a reading environment (mean=3.8 or 3.9) and support the reading processes at home (mean=3.9). They were aware of their roles to promote reading (mean=3.6) but they were less certain about the extent of their role modelling effect (SD=.8). It is in contrast with a conventional belief that socially deprived families should have lower confidence and participate less in children's reading. Following this line of thought, some questions can be asked: what were the sources of their self-efficacy to support the students despite their disadvantaged background? Why did the socially deprived parents in Hong Kong get involved in children's reading?

Sources of Self-Efficacy to Read with Children

In order to assist the children properly, parents need to have skills for supporting the reading process, for preparing a favourable environment and setting examples for their children to follow. More than 40 per cent of the interviewees acquired the techniques themselves, indicating that they mostly learnt from doing. Some parents told stories based on an understanding of the children's personality; some learnt from books or mass media; some experimented with the elder child(ren) in their families and others reflected upon the experience of reading with their siblings in the past.

> "I learn storytelling myself. I like to imitate the voices or read aloud even when I read alone. Probably it is because I read to my younger brother some years ago."

In fact, 25 per cent of interviewees claimed the people around them influenced their methods to read with their children. For example,

> "We read poems written in Tang dynasty. (Why do you think it is important?) A few of my Mainland Chinese friends use the same method. Their children read a lot."

On the other hand, only 13 per cent of interviewees learnt from the seminars organized by the external organizations. A unique example was a parent who wished to provide more support for her autistic son. He had been only interested in reading the texts in the past, irrespective of whether he could comprehend the meaning. After having the training, the mother learnt to choose English books without more than four difficult words on one page. This helped her a lot to screen the materials for the child.

The low level of participation in trainings can be accounted by two reasons. First, most of the interviewees had received education up to Secondary 3 and the children were still young. It was possible for the parents to assist them at this stage. Moreover, very specific knowledge or techniques was unnecessary for parent-child reading in the eyes of the caregivers. Their understanding about their children and the intimate parent-child relationship was adequate for nurturing reading interests. Therefore most parents learnt the techniques by reading, advanced their skills by practice, and then re-confirmed their beliefs by sharing with their peers (Bandura, 1989). As some parents said:

> "I learnt the techniques from the books about children's psychology, newspapers and chats with other parents."

> "I had no idea about the difference between reading aloud or telling stories in the past. I started with reading from word-to-word. My son reminded me to speak naturally when I told stories. He taught me!"

> "My friend told me that parents have to read with children; however, I haven't done enough. She has told stories every night since her son was in kindergarten."

In fact, parents were less confident to identify the needs of children for reading development (question 7, table 1). Nearly half of them were also uncertain or disagreed that they could be role models of their children (question 9, table 1). This reflects that parents had a restricted understanding about children's reading and the roles they could perform. Moreover, it is relatively new to convey the skills systematically to the Hong Kong families. Formal training offered to parents has been flourished only in the last ten years. As a result, the caregivers usually learnt the skills from various sources, rather than from external educational programmes such as those offered by schools and public libraries.

If the disadvantaged parents experienced difficulties in reading with their children, they tried to utilize their social resources to assist their children in the reading processes. Families could check the dictionaries when they did not know the pronunciations or meanings of certain words. If it still did not help, the less educated parents knew where they could get further assistance. Sources of support came from their relatives, friends, colleagues and neighbours. The reach-out behaviour could be explained by the Asian culture. Low-income parents were not necessarily deterred from getting involved by the limited resources and the education they had; rather some could effectively make use of the social network to help in the schooling of their children (Stevenson and Stigler, 1992). It also indicates how the Chinese tradition of valuing education influences parental support for the students (Lin, 1999; Lee, 1996).

> "He can get help from the senior students living in the neighbourhood. I can also ask my friends or other parents if I don't understand something."

> "I don't know the words and I cannot help him. He can ask his elder sisters if he comes across any difficulty. (What will happen if the sisters don't know?) The sisters have private tutor." (A parent who came from Mainland China and received primary education)

Nevertheless, the social support might not work in all cases, particularly when the collaborating communities shared similar cultural possessions and social networks. Disadvantaged parents could not only use self-learning and peer support to improve their understanding about parent-child reading. For example, some caregivers might have to invest a lot of resources to experiment and choose appropriate reading materials. The selection processes did not only depend on students' personal interests, but also parents' capabilities to identify their needs at different developmental stages. If the parents could learn from the schools and other external organizations, the problem might be lessened.

> "Learning how to select books is a tough process! When my elder daughter was small, I bought a lot of books. However, we did not have the time to read all of them. I just picked up any book and discussed with her disregarding the level. After understanding the child's interests and comprehension, I keep the appropriate books for my younger daughters."

Similarly, parents who borrowed books for the children experienced certain difficulties, which could leave a gap for the school to train the parents. A parent said:

> "Sometimes the teacher librarian recommends nice English books to my child. Unfortunately I cannot get similar ones in the public libraries because I may not know how to choose."

In summary, most disadvantaged parents were confident in their techniques to support students' reading at home. Since reading at the second grade was seen as 'elementary' compared to the amount of education they had received, parents usually got involved based on personal learning and their daily encounters with their children. Learning from peers was also popular. Attending seminars was treated as 'unnecessary' because the caregivers could obtain social support from elsewhere. Unfortunately, this limited the parents' understanding about parent-child reading, as exemplified by the case of selecting reading materials. This was also the reason why school support for parental involvement could be useful.

Supporting the Students to Read for Literacy and Academic Performance

In the previous section, the interviewees reported they read with the children to diagnose the words they did not understand. They also found reading important in providing opportunities for their children to imagine, think creatively and learn about judgment. On the other hand, reading for literacy and knowledge and for children's empowerment were the commonest objectives of giving the assistance. Adults who had received less education and/or had lower socio-economic status especially emphasized these goals. This belief became strong motivation for parental involvement and the origin of such belief will be discussed in the next section.

> "I was an illiterate in the past. Now I watch TV and read newspapers to learn. I wish my grandson to read more so that he can be more proficient in languages." (A parent who left school after Primary 6)

> "I lived in Indonesia some years ago but I could not receive any Chinese language education. However, I have to read Chinese menu in the restaurants and read the notices when I go shopping in Hong Kong. Therefore I always visit the library and read now...If my son reads more, his literacy can improve."

> "The Chinese language taught in this school is very difficult. There is a lot of reading comprehension in the examinations. If you don't read, you cannot achieve."

> "My relatives have a lot of books at home but they don't read with their children. The children don't have a habit to read and therefore they don't have a lot of knowledge."

The Roles of Parents

According to table 1, 71 per cent of the respondents believed that they played a role to cultivate children's reading habit (question 8). More than half thought they could set examples for the children to follow (question 9). However, 25 per cent were uncertain of making this claim. Similarly, the interviewees did not have very clear role concept and the specific ways they could help the students. Parents usually gave general answers such as their children could imitate them if they read themselves. As two parents said:

> "Family members have to read first. It is impossible to teach the children if we don't read."

> "I love reading a lot...I ask my younger daughter to sit next to us (mother and elder sister). She loves to be with us. She imitates what we do."

Culture as the Parental Motivation for Supporting Children to Read

Previous discussions show that most disadvantaged parents tried to support their children because of two reasons. They believed their children could have better language proficiency and academic performance if they read extensively. It was also their duties to assist them in reading. This section aims to explain how the Chinese culture, to a large extent, shapes these motivational beliefs.

Parental involvement in general has its cultural dimension. Parents getting involved at home can be seen as parenting, which is under the influence of the school, mass media and the groups for which the family belongs to. To a broader extent, these entities are shaped by the values, beliefs, social class and culture. Therefore parental involvement, especially home-based engagement, is partly constructed by culture. The values and norms of children's education are commonly shared in a given society. It determines short-term and long-term objectives of parents hold for their children and the ways the adults try to reach these goals. Chinese emphasize on the importance of education in bringing success of life (Lee, 1996). Learning for pleasure (and with fun) is more common in Western childrearing than in the East. On the contrary, Asian students are expected to work hard and perseverant so that they will become well educated, morally sound citizens (Bai, 2005). Personal success is not attributed to abilities; rather industry is the key to success.

At the same time, there are norms to define the child-rearing practices to secure this success. Parents have to provide the best conditions for children in learning, disregarding the social constraints they face (Lin, 1999). They are expected to provide the physical, psychological and economic conditions which are necessary for the children to survive in the society. Therefore it is not surprising that disadvantaged families would like to invest a lot of family spending on setting a study place at home, to provide private tuition and arrange extra-curricular activities. Chinese parents are particularly involved at home (Stevenson and Stigler, 1992, p.55).

Assisting Children to Read for Literacy and Academic Performance

It is common for the disadvantaged parents to emphasize academic performance in Western societies (Kohn, 1997; as cited by Lareau, 2000, p181). Sonnenschein (1997, as cited by Weigel, Martin, and Bennett, 2006) also pointed out the differences between the beliefs of high- and low-income families.

In assisting the literacy development of pre-school children, wealthy families tended to adopt an 'entertainment' approach in reading with the students; while the counterparts were more skill-oriented. Similar to Western families, Hong Kong parents of this study were found to support the children for the sake of children's empowerment; however, the emphasis was much stronger in the Chinese society.

Literacy education has been very important in the early Chinese history, which could be indicated by the names associated with education used at that time. For instance, elementary schooling was called as *shuxue* (書學; *shu* means books or texts), whereas the institutions were for learning characters (書館 *shuguan*). The contemporary teachers were language teachers (書師 *shushi*) (Bai, 2005, p.22).

Although instilling moral values had become more important than literacy in the later part of Chinese history, children still had to learn simple characters before they could read other Confucian classics (ibid, p.72). The frequent appearance of the term 'books' or 'texts' (書 *shu*) reflects the emphasis of language education in the culture. As part of literacy, reading is also valued in Confucianism. In a book called 'Reading Method' by a philosopher Zhu Xi in Song dynasty, intensive reading of text and commentary is the foundation of reflection, thinking and learning. People have to read with an open mind without bringing one's pre-occupations (Lee, 1996, p.35). Teachers were guided by traditional texts to teach rudimentary literacy skills and behaviour. Rituals for children also included instructions on reading and writing characters in the past (Bai, 2005, p.78).

In fact, many parent interviewees participated in this study mixed up reading and academic study. They treated reading books (in Chinese, 看書 *can shu*) equivalent to studying (讀書 *du shu*). As informed by the teacher librarians of the four schools in some informal conversations, most parents were 'traditional', 'realistic' and 'academic oriented'. They usually neglected other benefits of reading. They just thought if their children were proficient in reading, they would perform better in various subjects. Then it would be possible for them to have well-paid jobs in the future. This belief can be deeply rooted in a traditional statement 「書中自有黃金屋」, for which the direct translation means 'there is a golden house in books'. Reading is always related to jobs, prosperity and fortune in future. As a parent said:

"He is my son. I try to make it for his benefits…He may not have the same opportunity when he grows up."

The Confucian doctrines contributed to the establishment of the above claim. In Chinese culture, everyone is believed to be educable and literates can rule the country (Bai, 2005; Lee, 1996, p.37). The civil examination system (科舉 *ke ju*) established in Sui dynasty (隋 *sui*) was used to select the educated to serve the government. This belief was continuously reinforced by many classical dramas depicting hardworking, poor students were selected to work for governing positions. Education is always linked with fame, power and wealth. Under this notion, it was not surprising to have interviewees suggesting the schools to count book reports as part of the assessment. A language teacher even said unless the students were forced to read by the school, they would never experience the fun in reading.

This study reveals how the traditional beliefs drove the disadvantaged parents to be aware of their roles. In order to keep on the competitive edge, the families have to support the children to succeed in schooling. Parents having low socioeconomic status can have similar expectations and pay similar amount of effort as their counterparts. The extra investment can be paid off if the students can receive better education and have more valuable assets in life.

Reading with Children for Performing Parental Roles

The emphasis of role modelling in Asian education was already observed by the Western researchers in the 1970s. Stevenson and Stigler pointed out the major difference of 'modern' cultural symbols between the East and the West (1992). In the past, American children could imitate family or historic figures when they learnt. However, celebrities can be their role models nowadays just because of fame and wealth. Although Hong Kong has been westernized to a certain extent, figures with qualities such as industry and making good use of talents are still upheld morally. Parents are expected to teach these qualities not only by words, but also by the ways they behave. They have to set examples simple enough for children to understand, as well as to prepare an environment conducive to the learning processes.

The role modelling beliefs of Hong Kong parents are largely derived from the Confucian culture, which states all human are alike and born with good nature (人之初、性本善 *renzhichu xinbenshan*) (Bai, 2005). Practice (習 *xi*) of a child is continuously influenced by environmental factors such as the parents' attributes, socio-economic status, the education children receive and the social culture. In order to shape a child's personality, the family has to set up examples easy enough for him/her to follow. This is consistent with a concept called 'osmosis', which emphasizes the 'nurturance, interdependence, and close physical proximity' to prepare a readiness for the child to 'imitate, accept and internalize' the correct values (Hess and Azuma, 1991).

Role modelling beliefs can also be accounted by rite (禮 *li*). Rituals are the ideals of social norms which define one's social position. However, social classes in Confucianism does not mean social strata; rather they refer to the distinction between good and bad. It is regarded as a 'decorum' which provides an objective standard of conduct and governs social deportment and interpersonal relationship (Bai, 2005, p.68 and 69). A set of expected behaviour has to be internalized so that one would not lose face. In other words, parents have to behave according to the rites and teach the children the necessary skills and moral values. It is the adults' mistakes if they do not teach the children well ('To feed the body, not the mind – fathers, on you the blame!' - *Three Characters Classics*). This can also explain why some parents have started to read with their children even when they were babies.

Parents can influence the children a lot if they make reading a habit or an entertainment at leisure time. A number of interviewees read when they travelled to work, while some encouraged their children to bring reading materials when they dined in restaurants or even when they travelled abroad. Visits to library and bookstores could be a family activity on weekends.

> "If my daughter feels bored at home, I ask her to read the books we have borrowed or those we have at home."

> "My son may wish to buy some books. Therefore I ask him to save pocket money or win book coupons in competitions."

Moreover, it was important for the parents to reinforce good behaviour by reminding the children and recognizing their effort. For example, an interviewee thought children should not flip through the pages or view the pictures alone. Therefore she always reminded her son to understand the content while he reads. Another parent allowed her son who loved reading to read for five minutes if he finished a piece of homework.

In conclusion, Chinese culture, to a certain extent, shapes the beliefs of Hong Kong parents to support children's reading at home. Literacy, knowledge and examinations have been emphasized in the history for a long time. Reading is taken as a mechanism for academic advancement, rather than for entertainment or for fun. In order to make children more competitive in the future, parents are eager to carry out their duties according to their knowledge and experience.

Apart from empowering the children, Hong Kong parents are influenced by the Confucian doctrines of role modelling. Children are born to be ready for learning. Since the family is the first place of education, parents have to set examples simple enough for children to follow, as well as to convey their perceived values of reading through intense parent-child communications. If they fail to perform their roles, they would lose the respect in the community. In short, the caregivers have to provide the environment conducive to reading for the sake of children's benefits, role modelling and social expectations.

CONCLUSION

Regardless of the constraints they faced, most socially deprived parents of the second graders in Hong Kong were supportive in children' reading at home. The caregivers were eager to prepare an environment necessary to nurture reading interests and actually read with them. Their behaviour was found to be closely related to their self-efficacy beliefs and role awareness. They were confident in preparing a reading environment and providing assistance in the reading processes. This could be proven by the techniques they used in parent-child reading. The caregivers acquired the skills from parent-child interactions, self-study and their social networks. Even if they could not solve the problems themselves, they tried to utilize the resources available in the neighbourhood.

Nevertheless, the search for support was kept within the social circle of the family rather than from the larger community. As a result, some parents could have restricted understanding of parent-child reading and the roles they could perform. This implies strategies aiming to reduce their social constraints, strengthen the family environment and encourage school-based participation can make a difference in their competence. The association between school support and skill acquisition increases when children progress to higher grades. In a similar vein, primary schools can support children directly in literacy enhancement, as well as continue to promote parental involvement in reading. . A structured home-reading scheme can motivate less proficient parents to help their children at home (Nutbrown et al., 2005, p.22), or even bring the parents who rarely pay visits back to schools (Bloom, 1987).

This study also reveals how disadvantaged parents helped their children because of love and expectations. With a strong influence of Confucianism, reading was associated with language proficiency, knowledge, academic performance and children's future. Reading for fun and interests was treated as a less important goal. The parents could have ambiguous ideas about the roles they played and might be uncertain whether they could become role models. Nonetheless, they understood the importance of setting examples for children to imitate. The failure of performing this function would possibly imply a public disgrace. These beliefs, once again, were deeply rooted in the Chinese culture.

Similar to the comparative study carried out by Stevenson and Stigler (1992) for America and the Asian regions, this research uses a critical perspective to reveal how cultural norms shaped the landscape of student learning and parental involvement. It is worth noting that emphasizing role concept in children's literacy is not unique in Hong Kong. As evident from this research and some Western studies (Hoover-Dempsey et al., 2005; Nutbrown et al., 2005), both Eastern and Western caregivers can also set high expectations for their children to excel in schooling. Indeed, the use of Chinese culture and Confucianism to explain the pattern in Hong Kong does not intend to neglect the other factors affecting parents' decisions, or to ignore the effects of similar/different norms in various systems; rather it provides a holistic account of how parents responded to the socially embedded doctrines and perpetuated them through actions. When the region is gearing into globalization, traditional influence on family practices can change. A longitudinal study in the future may probably be useful to uncover the interacting, competing forces in bringing such changes.

REFERENCES

Bai, L. (2005). *Shaping the Ideal Child: Children and their Primers in Late Imperial China.* Hong Kong: The Chinese University Press.

Bandura, A. (1989). Regulation of Cognitive Processes Through Perceived Self-Efficacy. *Developmental Psychology*, 25(5), 729-735.

Bloom, W. (1987). Partnership with Parents in Reading. London: Hodder and Stoughton. CUHK The Chinese University of Hong Kong, (2010). The Results of Programme for International Student Assessment. Retrieved on December 8, 2010, from http://www.fed.cuhk.edu.hk/~hkpisa/events/2009/ files/PISA2009_Results_c.pdf

Coleman, J.S. (1994). Family, School and Social Capital. In. T. Husen, and T.N. Postlethwaite (Eds.), *The International Encyclopedia of Education* Vol.4 (2nd ed.). Oxford: Pergamon Press.

Davie, R., Butler, M., and Goldstein, H. (1972). *From Birth to Seven: the second report of the National Child Development Study* (1958 Cohort). London: Longman.

Dearing, E., McCartney, K., Weiss, H.B., Kreider, H., and Simplins, S. (2004). The promotive effects of family educational involvement for low-income children's literacy. *Journal of School Psychology*, 42, 445-460.

Education and Manpower Bureau (2006). Speech of the Permanent Secretary for Education and Manpower Bureau on the Conference 「學會閱讀：世界各地的先進經驗和香港小學生的表現」Retrieved on June 1, 2006, from http://www.emb.gov.hk/FileManager/TC/ Content_3990/psem speech0503.pdf

Education and Manpower Bureau (2002). Letter from the Permanent Secretary for Education and Manpower Bureau on "Promotion of Reading Culture in School". Retrieved on June 9, 2006, from http://www.emb.gov.hk/FileManager/TC/Content_ 3990/e.pdf

Hannon, P. (1987). A study of the effects of parental involvement in the teaching of reading on children's reading test performance. *British Journal of Educational Psychology*, 57, 56-72.

Hess, R. D., and Azuma, H. (1991). Cultural support for schooling: contrasts between Japan and the United States. Educational Researcher, 20(9), 2-12.

Ho, S.C. (2003) Students' Self-Esteem in an Asian Educational System: Contribution of Parental Involvement and Parental Investment. *The School Community Journal*, 13(1), 65-84.

Hoover-Dempsey, K., Walker, J., Sandler, H., Whetsel, D., Green, C., Wilkens, A., and Closson, K. (2005). Why Do Parents Become Involved? Research Findings and Implications. *The Elementary School Journal*, 106(2), 106-131.

Hong Kong Housing Authority (2010). Hong Kong Housing in Figures. Retrieved on November 30, 2010, from http://www.housingauthority.gov.hk/hdw/content/document/en/aboutus/resources/statistics/HIF2010.pdf.

Kellaghan, T. (1994). Family and Schooling. In. T. Husen, and T.N. Postlethwaite (Eds.), *The International Encyclopedia of Education* Vol.4 (2nd ed.). Oxford: Pergamon Press. pp.2250-2258.

Kirby, P. (1992). *Story Reading at Home and at School: Its Influence Upon Children's Early Literacy Growth. Reading*, 26(2), 7-12.

Lareau, A. (2000). *Home Advantage: Social Class and Parental Intervention in Elementary Education.* Oxford: Rowman and Littlefield Publishers, Inc.

Lee, W. O. (1996) The Cultural Context for Chinese Learners: Conceptions of Learning in the Confucian Tradition. In. D.A. Watkins, and J.B. Biggs (Eds.), The Chinese Learner: Cultural, Psychological and Contextual Influences. Hong Kong and Melbourne: CERC and ACER.

Lin, J. (1999) *Social Transformation and Private Education in China.* Westport: Praeger Publishers. Chp.3.

Loveday, E., and Simmons, K. (1988). Reading At Home: Does It Matter What Parents Do?. *Reading*, 22(2), 84-88.

Nutbrown, C., Hannon, P., and Morgan, A. (2005). *Early Literacy Work with Families – Policy, Practice and Research.* London: Sage Publications Ltd.

Pomerantz, F.K. (2001). Parent-Child Literacy Projects. In. D.B. Hiatt-Michael (Ed.), *Promising Practices for Family Involvement in Schools.* Connecticut: Information Age Publishing.

Radio Television Hong Kong RTHK (2003). Parent-Child Reading Survey in Hong Kong Families《香港家庭親子閱讀習慣調查》. Retrieved on August 31, 2008, from http://www.rthk.org.hk/press/chi/20030509_66_78201.html.

Sénéchal, M., and LeFevre, J. (2002). *Parental Involvement in the Development of Children's Reading Skill: A Five-year Longitudinal Study. Child Development*, 73(2), 445-460.

Stevenson, H. W., and Stigler, A.W. (1992). The learning gap: *why our schools are failing and what we can learn from Japanese and Chinese education.* London : Simon and Schuster.

Stuart, M., Dixon, M., Masterson, J., and Quinlan, P. (1998). Learning to read at home and at school. *British Journal of Educational Psychology*, 68, 3-14.

Tizard, B., and Hughes, M. (2002). Young Children Learning (2nd ed.). Oxford: Blackwell Publishing.

Tizard, J., Schofield, W.N., and Hewison, J. (1982). Collaboration between Teachers and Parents in Assisting Children's Reading. *British Journal of Educational Psychology*, 52, 1-15.

Weigel, D., Martin, S., and Bennett, K. (2006). Mothers' literacy beliefs: Connections with the home literacy environment and pre-school children's literacy development. *Journal of Early Childhood Literacy*, 6(2), 191-211.

In: Evidence-Based Education ISBN: 978-1-61324-927-7
Editors: D. Chun-Lok and V. Wang-Yan © 2012 Nova Science Publishers, Inc.

Chapter 5

RURAL ELEMENTARY SCHOOL SCIENCE TEACHER ATTITUDES TOWARDS VARYING PROFESSIONAL DEVELOPMENT STRATEGIES

Leonard A. Annetta, James Minogue, Michelle Cook, James A. Shymansky and Brandi Turmond
Department of Mathematics, College of Education,
North Carolina State University, NC, US

ABSTRACT

As part of a federally funded research initiative, elementary level science teachers' views regarding perceived effectiveness of four different professional development activities were investigated. Participants ($n=259$) from rural schools in the Midwestern United States participated in one of four different professional development (PD) activities: workshop, focus group, peer mentoring, and Interactive Television.

Following participation in one of the four PD activities, participants were asked to provide feedback about the PD activity by completing a 5-point Likert scale survey consisting of 9 items, to help better understand teacher attitudes towards the various PD strategies and the overall effectiveness of the PD in promoting teacher pedagogical content knowledge (PCK).

Study results indicated significant differences among teachers participating in the different PD activities in all of the nine post experience attitudinal-criteria.

INTRODUCTION

The focus of this research study was to affect local and systemic change in elementary science instruction by investing the effectiveness of various forms of professional development in enhancing teacher pedagogical content knowledge (PCK).

Through these professional development delivery strategies, teachers were exposed to rich content knowledge enhancement and ways in which they use that new knowledge to effectively teach the content.

Hence, the notion of PCK was pinnacle in this project. Over 1,300 teachers and more than 20,000 students in 38 school districts in the central region of the US were involved in this study, which targeted elementary science school teachers (grades 2-5) in traditionally underserved, rural school districts. Teachers were recruited through word of mouth and volunteered to participate in this project. This study provided an opportunity to research the efficacy of non-traditional or alternative professional development delivery strategies.

One of the central goals of the five-year *Science Co-op Project* was to enhance the pedagogical content knowledge (PCK) of the participating teachers through a series of summer workshops, school year support, and distance learning sessions. To this end, a *cascading leadership model* (Shymansky et al., 2004) served as the infrastructure of the project, with teachers that participated in the first year of the project becoming the lead or mentor teachers for the subsequent 4 years.

Each year involved another group of teachers from the respective 38 participating districts in varying professional development activities, with lead teachers from the first year leading the new cohorts of teachers, while university faculty in science and science education facilitated the four different professional development delivery strategies.

During the fourth year of the project, participating teachers' attitudes towards and perceived effectiveness of the professional development activity they participated in were explored to better understand which professional development strategies were most effective in enhancing the science pedagogical content knowledge of traditionally "hard to reach" teachers in rural settings. This study expands on previous studies that have explored the role PCK plays in professional development activities and the philosophical, logistical, and technological factors that impact how rural teachers perceive professional development.

THEORETICAL UNDERPINNINGS

Role of Pedagogical Content Knowledge

If educators are to challenge students to have a deeper understanding of the content and engage in high order thinking, they themselves need to have a thorough understanding of those content they are teaching and how to best teach the content to students (Enfield, 2000). Schneider and Krajcik (2002) described types of knowledge that teachers possess: content knowledge, pedagogical knowledge, and pedagogical content knowledge (PCK). The differentiation between the three being that content knowledge being a teacher's knowledge of their subject matter; pedagogical knowledge being a teacher's knowledge of things such as classroom management and organization; and pedagogical content knowledge being a teacher's knowledge of ways to present the content to students. In science, PCK would include a teacher's knowledge of the science content, knowledge of how to present that science content to students, and knowledge of ways to get students to think about science. Shulman (1986) defined PCK as the understanding of what makes the learning of specific topics easy or difficult for students and further elaborated on this definition (Shulman, 1987) by explaining that PCK encompasses knowledge of students' preconceptions, understanding and alternative conceptions of specific topics in the subject, knowledge of curriculum and standards, and instructional strategies and representations for teaching specific subject matter.

PCK is a hierarchy that encompasses general PCK, domain-specific PCK and topic-specific PCK (Veal, 1999). General PCK refers to the different content disciplines (math, science, history, etc.). Domain-specific PCK is a subtopic within these disciplines, such as science subtopics including chemistry, physics, biology, etc... Finally, topic-specific PCK refers to the specific topics within the domain, such that for physics, the topic-specific PCK would entail thermodynamics, optics, electricity and magnetism, and forces. Thus, teachers having topic-specific PCK would have an array of techniques and skills in both the general and domain-specific area.

Although expert teachers may possess PCK, studies indicate that preservice teachers and teachers in their early years of practice may lack PCK (Reynolds, 1995; Shulman, 1987). Some novice teachers have an expectation that there is a straightforward process for teaching science, much like the scientific method, and that if that process is followed, effective science instruction will result (Smith, 2000). Unfortunately, teaching and learning is not a straightforward process, as student learning is influenced by a number of factors, including teacher traits, skills and practices. That is, what a teacher needs to know to teach effectively is topic-specific pedagogical content. It is this PCK that is of paramount importance (Shymansky, 2000). Teachers that possess this type of knowledge are more readily able to diagnose student misunderstandings and subsequently employ appropriate strategies to combat these misunderstandings (Butler, 2003). It is this type of practice, that teachers are motivated to engage in the change process, and they begin to use student responses to inform instruction (Harcombe, 2001). It is hoped that through well-design science teacher professional development, PCK will improve and ultimately impact student learning. This may be especially true of traditionally underserved rural communities that house a population of teachers that have historically not received the same teacher development attention enjoyed by their urban and suburban counterparts.

Rural Populations and Teacher Professional Development

The term "underserved" is multifaceted when referring to most rural schools. Not only are these schools geographically isolated, but also in many cases these teachers must cope with poor text materials, as well as inadequate classrooms and labs (Lynch, 2000). A larger problem, endemic to the K-12 teaching profession, is the isolation of the classroom teacher. Most teachers in the US are isolated and, unlike other professionals, have little access to the resources they need to stay up to date in their fields. In contrast, teachers in other countries are provided far more paid time for planning and professional development, as indicated by a Web Based Education Commission (2000), in which Japanese teachers spent about 40 percent of their paid time on professional development and collaboration compared to 14 percent for their American counterparts. According to Vygotsky (as cited in Glasson, 1993), collaboration with other professionals allows for essential learner interactions and it has been suggested that professional development programs that allow teachers to work as teams are most successful (Rosenholtz, 1987). However, oftentimes rural schools are too isolated from other professionals to provide this needed collaboration (Renyi, 1996). Rural school systems are underserved not only by their isolation from other teachers but also by their isolation from research institutions (Williams, 1995). Due to this isolation, teachers in rural areas often seem "out of touch" with optimal teaching strategies, due to their inability to keep abreast of the most current research (Stephans, 1994). Rural schools by structure and philosophy often match the expectations and description of a learning community. Establishing a learning community in a rural school can create an atmosphere that encourages committed educators to grow through trust, respect, and collegiality (Haar, 2003). In rural Michigan for example, 102 teachers immersed in a professional development experience on constructivist pedagogy expressed the importance of community to overcome the apprehension to their changing pedagogy (Kinnucan-Welsch and Jenlink, 2001). The call for teachers to become "Highly Qualified" is daunting. Accomplishing this requires statewide collaboration among higher education, school districts, certification boards, and departments of education. Data from recent studies of teacher recruitment, retention, and professional development in Wyoming illustrates the dilemmas of trying to improve teacher quality in rural states with decreasing populations and resources (Holloway, 2002). Wyoming is only one example of the decreasing population and resource dilemma. A review of recent literature examined the growing shortage of qualified teachers, related to rising enrollments and high teacher turnover for rural schools in Oregon, Washington, and Montana (Boss, 2001). For rural schools to succeed, ongoing professional development is crucial. In the *Prairie Teachers Project*, it was reported rural schools that had ongoing professional development programs, supportive colleagues and administrators, and stable employment conditions were more likely to retain new teachers (Harris, 2001). A possible solution to the lack of professional development for rural teachers is to reach these teachers via distance education technologies. Part of the present study set out to investigate the effectiveness of teaching elementary school science teachers PCK through two-way videoconference delivery. The use of communication technologies, such as this, allows teachers to continue their education through professional development of science and to build collaborative learning networks (Williams, 1995). This is especially true for teachers in underserved rural areas who are oftentimes isolated from opportunities for professional growth (Renyi, 1996; Williams, 1995).

METHODOLOGY

Research Question

Although this project had large numbers of students, this evidenced-based chapter will look strictly at the impact the professional development models had on teachers. This study sought to examine whether differences existed among teacher attitudes towards varying professional development activities by exposing participants to one of the four different professional development delivery strategies detailed below:

1. Workshops: larger groups of teachers participated in professional development activities geared towards teacher planning and implementation of kit-based content (i.e. FOSS, STC, and Insights) into their classrooms, during which teachers were supervised and supported by leadership teams, field support staff, central project staff, and consulting experts.
2. Focus Groups: smaller groups of teachers engaged in 1 to 8 hour sessions in which teachers raised questions and issues about one or more *Teacher Resource Books* (TRB) to other teachers, leadership team members, or outside consultants. The TRB's were teacher created resource books that described the adaptations made to the recommended activities provided by the teacher guides in the science kits. During focus group sessions, teachers studied not only the science component of their curriculum, but also how the science component could relate to other areas of the elementary curriculum.
3. Peer Mentoring: one or more teachers having two or three years experience with project activities provided assistance to one or two other teachers to help those teachers develop the necessary skills associated with the learning goals of the professional development activities. Frequently during peer mentoring teachers would observe a lesson (live or videotaped) and analyze the lesson using a modification of the *Horizon Research Incorporated* (HRI) observation form provided by NSF.
4. Interactive Television (ITV) Sessions: teachers participated in a three-hour distance education session, in which a practicing content expert described his/her work experience for about 30-45 minutes as it related to one or more of the FOSS, STC, and/or Insights kits. The content expert then led a live QandA session with a scientist for the

remainder of the three-hour session, during which there was live exchange of classroom application ideas among participants at different ITV sites (lead by the content expert and project staff), and discussion of classroom implications among teachers at each site (lead by the district leadership team). Teachers participating in the ITV session were given brief biographies of the session presenters and session outlines at least one week prior to the session and required to submit questions related to the topic that were either their students' questions or their own. Questions were then given to the presenter to help the presenter gear the session to the background and interests of participants.

To this end, the research question became: Where there difference among teacher attitudes toward varying professional development when they participated in different kinds of delivery strategies?

Instrument

All participating teachers completed a post-experience attitudinal survey, the aim of which was to ascertain teacher attitudes regarding the effectiveness and potential impact of the professional development activities on their actual teaching practices.

The self-report 5-point Likert type survey had 9-items to which respondents chose either 1= strongly disagree, 2= disagree, 3= neutral, 4= agree, or 5= strongly agree. Teachers could also choose "NA" if they felt that particular item was not appropriate for the professional development activity they experienced. Survey items are listed below:

1. The content of the activity was important to me.
2. The content of the activity fit with district needs.
3. The format of the activity was appropriate.
4. My understanding of science was increased.
5. My understanding of how to teach science was increased.
6. My understanding of how children learn was increased.
7. I learned ways to connect science to other curricular areas.
8. The activity helped me to adapt the kit to my classroom.
9. I feel better prepared to teach science after this activity.

Sample

Of the 1350 surveys submitted, a subsample of 259 surveys were purposefully selected because that was number of teachers and the frequency of the different professional development activities varied over the course of the school year. This sampling method was chosen because the same 259 teacher participants were actively engaged in all four-delivery strategies. Therefore, 259 teachers were sampled from the 4 professional development activities and distributed evenly based on their experience in the first four years of the project.

Analysis

Initial data analysis consisted of analyzing survey responses for each survey item individually using descriptive statistics, namely the mean, median, mode, response frequency and percentages.

Since the data was considered to be ordinal in nature, nonparametric inferential statistics were employed to examine whether or not statistically significant attitudinal differences existed among the teachers participating in the different professional development activities.

Specifically, Kruskal Wallis H-tests were conducted for each survey item to determine if participants' responses differed across the four types of professional development activities. An alpha level of .05 was used in all statistical procedures. The survey's internal consistency was assessed using a Cronbach's alpha test which produced a reliability coefficient of .87.

FINDINGS

Table 1. shows the descriptive statistics and frequency distribution of the survey responses for all teacher surveys (n=259) included in the data analysis. The results of the Kruskal Wallis H-tests (Table 2) suggest that there are statistically significant differences between the four groups of respondents on all nine survey items. The size of the mean ranks is deemed indicative of the level of agreement for the respondents; that is, the greater the mean rank, the greater the level of agreement with respect to each survey item.

An examination of Table 2 shows that the ITV group's mean ranks were the lowest on all but one item (*My understanding of science was increased*).

Table 1. Descriptive Statistics for Survey Responses

Item	Mean	Median	Mode	Strongly Disagree	Disagree	Neutral	Agree	Strongly Agree	NA
1	4.45	5.00	5.00	0 (0)	3 (1.2)	14 (5.4)	105 (40.4)	137 (52.7)	0 (0)
2	4.63	5.00	5.00	0 (0)	1 (0.4)	14 (5.4)	64 (24.6)	180 (69.2)	0 (0)
3	4.54	5.00	5.00	4 (1.5)	0 (0)	14 (5.4)	76 (29.2)	165 (63.5)	0 (0)
4	4.10	4.00	4.00	3 (1.2)	9 (3.5)	41 (15.8)	106 (40.8)	94 (36.2)	6 (2.7)
5	4.04	4.00	4.00	3 (1.2)	5 (1.9)	53 (20.4)	108 (41.5)	82 (31.5)	8 (3.5)
6	3.91	4.00	4.00	2 (0.8)	11 (4.2)	61 (23.5)	109 (41.9)	67 (25.8)	9 (3.8)
7	4.12	4.00	5.00	3 (1.2)	9 (3.5)	47 (18.1)	86 (33.1)	103 (39.6)	11 (4.6)
8	3.92	4.00	4.00	12 (4.6)	9 (3.5)	25 (9.6)	76 (29.2)	64 (24.6)	73 (28.5)
9	3.91	4.00	4.00	3 (1.2)	12 (4.6)	53 (20.4)	98 (37.7)	66 (25.4)	27 (10.8)

Note: Responses were on a 5-point Likert scale (1 = strongly disagree, 5 = strongly agree).
Response Frequency (%).
($n = 259$).

Table 2. Comparison of Survey Responses Across the Types of Professional Development

Item	Workshop ($n = 65$) Mean Rank	ITV ($n = 74$) Mean Rank	Focus Group ($n = 82$) Mean Rank	Mentoring ($n = 38$) Mean Rank	Df	χ^2	p
1	161.22	98.47	138.63	119.38	3	33.423	.000**
2	152.27	97.47	152.66	104.26	3	48.226	.000**
3	156.56	94.95	145.96	116.75	3	40.765	.000**
4	151.93	121.55	119.48	110.43	3	12.082	.007**
5	150.20	106.67	127.42	119.46	3	14.461	.002**
6	160.51	82.94	129.91	139.28	3	47.678	.000**
7	152.11	80.00	141.43	116.13	3	44.652	.000**
8	117.84	63.19	111.49	83.85	3	38.035	.002**
9	128.45	94.61	131.34	115.27	3	14.538	.000**

Note: Responses were on a 5-point Likert scale (1 = strongly disagree, 5 = strongly agree).
The Kruskal Wallis H test was used to compare groups.
**$p < .05$.

Conversely, the workshop group's mean ranks were the highest on all survey questions except for items 2 and 9 (*The content of the activity fit with district needs* and *I feel better prepared to teach science after this activity*). In fact, a trend can be seen in 5 of the 9 items whereby the mean rank of the workshop group was the highest, followed by the focus group, the peer mentored group, and the ITV group.

DISCUSSION

The results presented here represent an initial attempt to characterize teacher attitudes towards varying modes of professional develop; however, the discussion of the findings of the study is not without its limitations. This study relied on self-report data and there is the realization that what the participants indicated on the survey and what the participants actually do in the classroom may not always be congruent. Future efforts will center on establishing how these varying forms of professional development activities influence not only teacher attitudes, but also their actions. In spite of the this limitation, the preliminary findings from this study can help to shed light on how teachers perceive and receive professional development activities delivered through different modes, including workshop, ITV, focus group, and mentoring.

Below is a description of each of the different professional development activities and a discussion of factors that may have influenced teachers' self-reported attitudes about that particular professional development activity, with an examination of participants' relatively poor attitudes toward the ITV sessions, and general recommendations regarding the planning and delivery of science teaching professional development activities.

WORKSHOP

The purpose of this culminating project was to enhance the science pedagogical content knowledge (PCK) of elementary teachers teaching in rural settings. Although the driving force behind each of the four professional development delivery strategies was increasing teacher PCK, it seems that this was best achieved through the use of workshop style professional development activities. More precisely, it was these teachers that reported the highest levels of agreement to the questions that asked if they felt that their *understandings of science* (item #4) and *how to teach science* (item #5) increased, the crux of PCK. It should be added that no differences in the level of agreement to these two survey items were found among the other three presentation modes.

This finding may be in part due to teachers' prior experience and level of comfort with this type of professional development. Here, larger groups of teachers were able to work with colleagues (under the guidance of leadership teams, field support staff, central project staff, and/or consulting experts) on ways to implement the kit-based content into their classrooms. It may be that this mode of professional development was best able to establish a learning community in these rural schools and created an atmosphere that encouraged committed educators to grow through trust, respect, and collegiality (Haar, 2003).

Focus Group

Related to this point is that focus group participants reported levels of agreement that were very similar to that of the workshop group on several items, namely their self-perceived *ability to connect science to other curricular areas* (item #7) and *adapt kit materials*, (item #8) as well as in their assessment of the *importance* (item #1) and *appropriateness of the activities* (item # 3). This format, like that of the workshop, allowed practicing teachers to work as teams to collaborate and share ideas regarding the realities of inquiry-based instruction (Rosenholtz, 1987). Here, small groups of teachers and leadership team members were able to confront reform efforts by sharing pedagogical strategies, discussing content, and collaborating on practical problem solving. This in turn may have resulted in a better understanding of student needs, curricular demands, and ultimately a feeling that the current science education reform efforts are worthwhile (Garet, 2001; Lieberman, 1992).

Peer Mentoring

A *cascading leadership model* was used in this project in hopes of reducing intimidation and/or anxiety that teachers sometimes report when working with university faculty and scientists. Previous anecdotal analysis of the project participants' attitudes provides another possible explanation for the observed differences. These elementary school teachers had a common apprehension toward interacting with scientists and university science educators. As is often the case, scientists are intimidating to those who don't speak the "science language" and who have not had a strong science background. This apprehension is especially true with rural teachers who have very little, if any, experience working closely with university faculty. It was thought that by allowing teachers to "teacher each other" in peer mentoring groups, improved attitudes towards and increased levels of understanding of science instruction would be found. The results of this exploratory study suggest that this did not occur. In fact respondents from the peer mentoring group reported relatively low levels of agreement on all of the survey items. The only group that reported lower levels of agreement was the ITV participants, a finding discussed further below. Possible explanations for this finding abound, but lie beyond the scope of this present chapter. It can be surmised, however, that a lack of training for the mentor teachers and the lack of fostering the relationship between the two groups may have contributed to this results. Let it suffice to say that more research into the dynamics of teacher led professional development activities is warranted, but the limited success of the *Peer Mentoring* format seen here can be reasonably attributed to the lack of opportunities for collaboration and sharing of ideas that made the workshops and focus groups successful.

INTERACTIVE TELEVISION

The notion of "comfort level" may help explain why the technology rich workshop environment of ITV was viewed so unfavorably by its participants. Although ITV and workshops were the two original professional development activities in the project, the sustained exposure to ITV showed no positive affect on teacher attitudes. The proposal of ITV for the rural teaching communities focused on the possibility of bridging the gap between scientists, science educators and elementary school science teachers. The comfort level, and subsequent attitudes toward the ITV experience varied throughout the first four years of this project. The variance may be explained by the teachers not wanting to spend extra time after school hearing something they already knew or hearing something they didn't completely understand. Although the scientists who presented the ITV sessions were informed about the characteristics and needs of their audience, this may not have been enough. It may take a special approach to deliver science content in a manner in which teachers believe that they are getting something out of the PD that they can use in their classrooms. Admittedly, the scientists were not coached on how to deliver science content from a distance and this too could have been a contributing factor to the results. Further, it get be inferred that elementary teachers have a natural trepidation of science and thus these sessions may have even further enhanced that trepidation. Ultimately that is what teachers want and need and it is what faculty who provide science teacher professional development should be alerted to. That is, provide professional development activities that provide teachers with materials, ideas, and understandings that they can take with them and directly apply to their classroom practice.

Unfortunately this was not always the case as scientists in years 1 and 2 often got off on tangents and forgot who their audiences were and thus the attitudes toward the ITV sessions were lower than the workshops and peer mentoring. It is important to note that scientists were not coached on the audience during the first year, thus the leadership teachers gained a negative attitude toward ITV. This negativity might have cascaded through the next 3 years and on to the new teacher groups as they entered the project.

RECOMMENDATIONS

The preliminary findings of this study can be used to better design and deliver professional development to elementary level science teachers, in order to better meet their needs and teaching goals, as well help them work more efficiently towards achieving the goals of science education reform. To improve teacher attitudes toward the perceived effectiveness of science professional development, the person(s) presenting the material needs to not only be an expert on science content, but more importantly on pedagogical content knowledge (PCK). Additionally, it may be that professional development formats that create and cultivate a learning community in which practicing teachers and experts can work in collaborative teams is a more effective professional development strategy that can increase teacher PCK and support the goals of current science education reform efforts.

The *National Science Foundation* and others strongly support the interaction of teachers and scientists. This is a crucial marriage of minds, if science education is to succeed in the near future. However, this is where the science educator needs to be the conduit between the two groups. Perhaps technology can serve as this conduit. ITV, in the form of 2-way compressed audio and video may be one viable candidate. Although the current study did not support this finding, the use of this communication technology showed more positive science learning effects on teachers in another study investigating science learning between ITV, web instruction, and videotape delivery modes (Annetta and Shymansky, 2006). The problem that persisted in terms of teacher attitudes toward ITV as a professional development activity was due in large part to the aforementioned communication barrier between the content deliver and the audience.

It is has become generally accepted that practicing teachers need continual sustained professional development in science content, but we are beginning to realize that the methods of delivering that professional development is a nuanced art form. It is a complex endeavor that, at a minimum, must account for peer group dynamics, teachers' personal preferences, individual comfort levels, and professional needs.

REFERENCES

American Association for the Advancement of Science. (1993). *Benchmarks for Science Literacy*. New York, NY: Oxford University Press.

Annetta, L.A., and Shymansky, J.A. (2006) The Effect Three Distance Education Strategies have on Science Learning for Rural Elementary School Teachers In A Professional Development Project. *Journal of Research in Science Teaching*, 43 (10), 1019-1039.

Boss, S. (2001). Facing the Future. *Northwest Education,* 7(2), 2-9,41.

Bruner, J. S. (1960). *Then Process of Education*. Cambridge, MA: Harvard University Press.

Butler, S. (2003, March). *Process vs. science content knowledge of middle school students constructing contour maps: A spatial, inquiry-based task*. Paper presented at the Annual Meeting of the National Association for Research in Science Teaching, Philadelphia, PA.

Enfield, M. (2000). *Content and pedagogy: Intersection in the NSTA standards for science teacher education*. Retrieved May 3, 2005, from http://www.msu.edu/~dugganha/PCK.htm

Garet, M. S., Porter, A.C., Desimone, L., Birman, B.F. and Suk Yoon, K. (2001). What makes professional development effective? Results from a national sample of teachers. *American Education Research Journal, 38*, 915-946.

Glasson, G., and Lalik, R. (1993). Reinterpreting the learning cycle from a social constructivist perspective: A qualitative study of teachers' beliefs and practices. *Journal of Research in Science Teaching, 30*(2), 187-207.

Haar, J. M. (2003). Providing Professional Development and Team Approaches to Guidance. *Rural Educator, 25*(1), 30-35.

Harcombe, E. S. (2001). *Science teaching, science learning.* New York: Teachers College Press.

Harris, M. M. (2001). Lessons from Prairie Teachers. *Action in Teacher Education, 23*(1), 19-26.

Holloway, D. L. (2002). Using Research To Ensure Quality Teaching in Rural Schools. *Journal of Research in Rural Education, 17*(3), 138-153.

Kinnucan-Welsch, K., and Jenlink, P. M. (2001). Stories of Supporting Constructivist Pedagogy through Community. *Alberta Journal of Educational Research, 47*(4), 294-308.

Lieberman, A., and McLaughlin, M.W. (1992). Networks for educational change: powerful and problematic. *Phi Delta Kappan, 73*, 673-677.

Lynch, S. (2000). *Equity and Science Education Reform: Listening to our better angels.* Mahwah, NJ: Lawrence Erlbaum and Associates.

Renyi, J. (1996). Teachers take charge of their learning. *Transforming professional development for student success [and] executive summary.* ERIC Document Reproduction Service, No. ED 401 251.

Reynolds, A. (1995). The knowledge base for beginning teachers: Education professionals' expectations versus research findings on learning to teach. *Elementary School Journal, 95*(3), 199-221.

Rosenholtz, S.J. (1987) Education reform strategies: Will they increase teacher commitment? *American Journal of Education*, 95, 534-562.

Rosenholtz, S. J. (1989). *Teachers' workplace: The social organization of schools.* New York: Longman.

Schneider, R., and Krajcik, J. (2002). Supporting science teacher learning: The role of educative curriculum materials. *Journal of Science Teacher Education, 13*(3), 221-245.

Shulman, L. S. (1986). Those who understand: knowledge growth in teaching. *Educational Researcher, 15*(2), 4-14.

Shulman, L. S. (1987). Knowledge and teaching: Foundations of the new reform. *Harvard Educational Review, 57*(1), 1-22.

Shymansky, J. A. (2000). *The role of student outcome data in teacher certification.* Paper presented at the National Science Council ROC (D), Taipei.

Shymansky, J.A., Yore, L.D., and Anderson, J.O. (2004). Impact of a School District's Science Reform Effort on the Achievement and Attitudes of Third- and Fourth-Grade Students. *Journal of Research in Science Teaching*, 41, 771-790.

Smith, D. C. (2000). Content and pedagogical content knowledge for elementary science teacher educators: Knowing our students. *Journal of Science Teacher Education, 11*(1), 27-46.

Stephans, J. (1994). *Targeting Students' Misconceptions: Physical Science Activities Using the Conceptual Change Model.* Riverview, FL: Idea Factory.

The National Commission on Teaching and America's Future. (1996). *What Matters Most: teaching for America's Future.*

Veal, W. R., and Makinster, J.G. (1999). Pedagogical content knowledge taxonomies. *Electronic Journal of Science Education, 3*(4).

Web Based Education Commission. (2000). *The Power of the Internet for Learning: Moving from Promise to Practice.* Washington, D.C.

Williams, E. (1995). Distance education as a future trend for pre and inservice education. ERIC Document Reproduction Services, No. 381 563.

In: Evidence-Based Education
Editors: D. Chun-Lok and V. Wang-Yan © 2012 Nova Science Publishers, Inc.
ISBN: 978-1-61324-927-7

Chapter 6

AN INVESTIGATION OF KOREAN GIFTED EDUCATION TEACHERS' VIEWS ON LEADERSHIP

Seung Hee Oh
Korea Baptist Theological University, Korea

Leadership skills have often been closely related to giftedness in giftedness research. The relationship between the concept of leadership and giftedness was made evident in the 'Marland Report' (U.S. Commissioner of Education, 1972). The federal definition of giftedness highlighted that gifted students could be defined as those who have leadership ability amongst other abilities:

> "Children capable of high performance include those with demonstrated achievement and/or potential ability in any of the following areas, singly or in combination: 1) general intellectual ability, 2) specific academic aptitude, 3) creative or productive thinking, 4) leadership ability, 5) visual or performing arts, 6) psychomotor ability (Marland, 1972, p. 2).

This definition emphasised the significance of leadership ability in gifted students, and was later used as the prototype for definitions of leadership adopted by most states of the US (Gallagher, Weiss, Oglesby, and Thomas, 1983). As a consequence of the seminal definition of giftedness, "leadership potential as one manifestation of giftedness is [now] commonly referred to in international descriptions of gifted students" (Cawood, 1984, p. 2).

The Korean government also stated that one of the main reasons for conducting gifted education was to develop new leaders in various fields. It stated that,

> ...in developing the gifted children's potentials to the best we can, these children will be able to grow towards self-actualisation and in every aspect of our society; they will be able to exhibit their abilities as leaders working towards national development and humanity (M. Kim, 2004, p. 30).

This view is complemented by the belief held in the Korean culture that a gifted child is a potential leader in society or in a particular subject area. Despite the belief that gifted children will grow up to become local or national leaders, in reality, due to the current Korean educational system which overly emphasizes knowledge-based education, little attention has been paid for the development of gifted students in any other way than academic. Therefore, the Korean government has not been able to identify nor develop a leadership scheme for gifted children thus far.

Thus, the focus of this study was to explore the views of Korean gifted teachers on leadership and gifted education. The research study aimed to find out how teachers understood the relationship between giftedness and leadership and furthermore, whether there was a demand for leadership education in gifted students. Moreover, what teachers understood as the adequacy of the current provisions as well as the suggested necessary components and characteristics of gifted curricula were also investigated.

METHODOLOGY

In order to gain in-depth knowledge of the teachers' perspectives as well as the socio-cultural context, the qualitative evidence of in-depth interviews were used with Korean gifted education teachers.

All the Korean schools are divided in terms of giftedness and age. Within the divided groups of schools, a set number of mainstream schools which offered gifted programmes and Centres for the Gifted within the areas near the South Korean capitol, the Seoul region, and the Gyeonggi province which surrounds the capitol area were considered for random sampling. The reason why Gyeonggi province and the Seoul area were chosen for this study was because gifted education is actively implemented in these areas.

From these schools, two teachers of gifted students were chosen at random for in-depth interviews. The Director of Korean Educational Development Institute was also specifically chosen as the third interviewee in order to gain the perspective of a specialist researcher of Korean gifted education. For this study, these three participants were selected and interviewed at length and depth for a detailed understanding and insights into the gifted education system within the Korean cultural context with particular emphasis on leadership development from the perspectives of teachers currently teaching in Korean schools as well as from an expert researcher in the field in Korea. The reasons for the limited selection of the interviewees was firstly due to the in-depth nature of the interviews conducted; in order to gain a thorough awareness of their views and teaching experiences, the number of interviewees were limited for more time to be spent with each interviewee. Secondly, there are not many researchers of gifted education in South Korea due to the early nature of the research field in the country. Hence, arguably the most senior researcher in the subject area was chosen in order to better comprehend the South Korean context of leadership development in gifted education setting.

In this research study, semi-structured interviews were conducted as it is more structured than an open conversation, but is more open than a strictly structured interview. In this type of interview, digressions were allowed for a deeper understanding of the topic (Berg, 2001). These types of interviews were conducted and analysed inductively using grounded theory throughout. Hence, this type of interviewing suits the data collection needed to answer research questions which are of a more causal nature, requiring more of in-depth perspectives on leadership and gifted education. However, there are disadvantages in the use of semi-structured interviews as it 'involves a complex set of social relationships that can contaminate the final product' (Verma and Mallick, 1999, p.128).

RELIABILITY AND VALIDITY

Concerning the interviews, Silverman (1993) argued that structure in interviews was one way to increase reliability (as cited in Cohen et al., 2000, p. 121). Therefore, the semi-structured nature of the interviews where "same format and sequence of words and questions" (p. 121) used to guide the interview improved its reliability. The teacher interviews were conducted over the telephone, possibly increasing reliability by encouraging the respondents to express opinions which they may not normally express if approached in person. Conversely, the disclosure of their names in the research could be a threat to the reliability of the interviews as it may lead to alterations in their replies due to social desirability. Nevertheless, the interviewees were asked whether they wished to disclose their names prior to conducting the interviews. In the case of validity, validity is increased by minimizing the amount of bias involved in the interview process. The use of leading questions was avoided in the compilation of the questions asked during the interviews. However, there are still some remaining issues concerning validity: as the researcher was in the presence of one of the participants during the interview, actions of the researcher might lead the participant to say things they believe the researcher would like (Cohen et al., 2000). There may also be gender, age and ethnicity differences between the interviewee and the interviewer which may affect the interview content.

Nevertheless, in sum, it is acknowledged that it is impossible to completely eradicate all threats to reliability and validity but many lengths were taken to maximise the reliability and validity of the two measures used in this research.

ETHICAL CONSIDERATIONS

The three participants were fully explained the details of the interviews and were ensured of their confidentiality, should they wish to remain anonymous. They were further informed that the written records would be kept of the interview for research purposes. They were also informed of their right to withdraw and leave any questions unanswered. All three participants offered verbal consent to interview participation and agreed in the disclosure of their names, positions and interview contents.

RESULTS

The interviews were semi-structured with some key questions, of which answers are summarised as follows. However, due to the in-depth and open nature of the interviews, there were many digressions and discussions of further information regarding their opinions on the current leadership development in gifted education in the South Korean context which will be reviewed in the Discussion and Analysis section of the chapter.

A. Interviews with Two Teachers

The interviewees were current Korean primary school teachers who also lead gifted students' classes in their own schools.

1. What do you think is the most urgent necessity in the Korean gifted education situation, taking into account of the fact that gifted education is recently becoming popular in Korea recently?

When asked the above question, the teachers provided 4 main suggestions. Firstly, they believed that in order for gifted education to develop, teachers should be trained in gifted education to prepare themselves for the gifted classes. Secondly, it was pointed out that a correct and accurate understanding of gifted students should be taught to teachers and parents. Thirdly, they expressed a need to recognise gifted education as a way for students to grow as humans and leaders rather than a way to accelerate and increase knowledge. Fourthly, one of the teachers said that there are too many pupils in one class for the teachers to teach effectively. This is the case in average classes as well as the gifted classes in Korea. Hence, it is nearly impossible for teachers to have any type of individual mentoring system with the students.

2. a) Do you have any moral education or character-building education in your school? Do you have special programmes for moral education in your school?

When asked, the two teachers replied that their school do not have separate leadership training programmes. One of the teachers said that in their school, the teachers individually try to incorporate some leadership education during mathematics and sciences lessons.

2. b) Do you find it hard to prepare for moral and character-building programmes by yourself?

Following on from the previous question, as one of the teachers stated that in their school, teachers individually prepare ways to incorporate leadership education in their typical teaching schedules, this question aimed to find out what the difficulties were in personally preparing for moral and character-building programmes.

When asked, one teacher admitted that it was a challenging task to handle moral programmes by themselves and resorted to enrolling into a graduate school by taking evening classes to learn more about leadership education. The teacher expressed a desire to research more in this area and is now working towards a Masters degree. On the other hand, the other teacher stated that moral education was initiated in their school, 3 years ago and they have 2-3 hours of moral education sessions per week. However, the teacher argued that this is too short a period to satisfy the gifted students' desires to know more about morality and ethics.

3. What is your opinion on whether being gifted and being a leader is the same or different?

In order to explore the relationship between leadership and giftedness further, this question was asked and the two teachers gave contrasting views. One teacher insisted that gifted students were also leaders as it was stated: "In Korea, when we think of gifted students, we see them as future leaders. We think that they are intelligent and clever, so for them to become leaders in their own fields is natural." Evidently, many Koreans relate giftedness with leadership skills. However, the other teacher believed that giftedness and leadership is not related as it was stated: "In my opinion, gifted children have a tendency to be self-absorbed, so this is the complete opposite of leadership characteristics. A leader should be able to care for others, sometime even before themselves. In this sense, it is very difficult to link giftedness with leadership skills."

4. What plans do you have in the future as a gifted education programme teacher? Is there anything else you would like to add?

In this question, the teachers' future aspirations for gifted education were asked, also providing them an opportunity to add any extra information. When asked, both teachers mentioned how gifted students should be developed to become leaders in societies as the two teachers responded:

> "Gifted students cannot merely have knowledge or talents, but should grow up and develop as a human being. This is the only way they will be able

to contribute towards society in the future. I feel the need to help gifted students to become true leaders with good manners and the desire to serve others."

"I would like to become a teacher who will be able to fulfil the students' learning desire and respond to their needs. I will also try to help them to be able to contribute as a leader towards the society or field that they will be in."

B. Interview with the Director of Education

The interview held on 20 August, 2005 with Dr. Meesook Kim, the Director of the Korean Office of Foundation and Policy. She is also part of the National Research Centre on Gifted and Talented Education and the Korean Educational Development Institute. Similar questions as the interviews described above with two gifted education teachers were asked so that a greater insight into gifted and leadership education can be seen from the perspective of a Korean educational expert.

1. What do you think is the most urgent necessity in the Korean gifted education situation, taking into account of the fact that gifted education is recently becoming popular in Korea?

In reply to this question, Kim emphasised the need for further research as she said,

"Since 2002, the Korean government designated and supported Centres of the Gifted and the National Research Centre on Gifted Education; however, because we cannot depend solely on foreign research results, we feel the need for research in gifted education specifically in the Korean culture and education."

2. What specific area of research are you focusing on recently?

This question was asked to find out the trend in Korean gifted education research at that time. She summarised the previous research that had been conducted and the importance of leadership research as she said,

"In 2003, we focused our research on gifted elementary school children's cognitive and affective characteristics and guiding strategies. In 2004, we put emphasis on cognitive and affective characteristics of and teaching strategies for the Korean junior high school gifted students. As the result of the research, we found that gifted students are extremely creative, have lots of interest in other people, have problem solving skills and leadership skills. This is why this year we are researching on methods of improving their creative problem solving skills, and strategies to develop their leadership skills."

3. What is your opinion on whether being gifted and being a leader is the same or different?

The view of a Korean researcher on the relationship between leadership and giftedness was sought in asking this question. She emphasised the significance of leadership in gifted education as she replied,

"In Korean society, it is difficult to disassociate giftedness and leadership. We all tend to believe that gifted students will develop to be our future leaders. Although there are gifted students who are gifted only in a single area, we recognise and hope that they will become leaders in their own fields. Therefore, in the next few years, our centre is planning to search for methods to develop gifted students as leaders."

4. What do you think is of most importance in educating gifted students as leaders?

When asked what she believed was most important in leadership gifted education, Kim believed that moral and character-building education was the most important aspect in teaching gifted students about leadership as she stated, "first of all, moral education and character-building education are important for leadership education. In order to contribute back to society what they received through their education, they should be able to think of others, respect people and have a desire to serve others in leadership."

5. What kind of suggestions do you have as a pioneering gifted education researcher in Korea?

As gifted education research only started recently in Korea, any advice for current researchers of Korean gifted education researchers was sought. She emphasised the need for further research as she said, "as researchers in gifted education which recently began in Korea, those with interest in this area should work hard with a pioneering mission. Because there are so many more things to research about, those who are ready with a desire to research in this area, or those who have studied this area abroad should take charge in conducting gifted education research."

DISCUSSION AND ANALYSIS

The analyses of the interviews were conducted using open-coding, axial coding and selective coding developed in grounded theory (Glaser and Strauss, 1967). In this section, the main findings from the interviews are summarised and discussed.

Korean Gifted Education Situation

a. Lack of Variety of Subjects in Gifted Education

The responses collected from the interviews emphasise the main problem in Korean gifted education is that there is a lack of variety in the subjects they offer to gifted students. The current gifted education given in Korea mainly deals with mathematics and the sciences. Due to the lack of variety in the subjects available in gifted education, the humanities and the other subjects are often neglected (Y. E. Kim, 2000, p. 31). Such overemphasis aided the development of modern scientific technology in Korea. Although the level of teaching in these areas is not yet satisfactory, those receiving science and mathematics gifted education are receiving education that is suitable for their talents and needs.

However, those with talents in music or art are being educated in independent and private institutions (S. H. Cho, 2000, p. 18). According to research in 2003, 0.28% of the students in Korea are receiving gifted education. Of these 21,616 students, 82% of them were found to be mathematics or science gifted. Only the remaining 18% were receiving gifted education in the arts, English and Information Technology (Suh et. al., 2003, p. 2).

The reason for the lack of provision for gifted education in other fields such as the arts and the humanities is mainly because the government does not feel as much need for them as it does for mathematics and the sciences as mathematics and the sciences work to strengthen the nation's economy. Hence, any investment in the education of mathematics and the sciences is seen as a necessary action for the development of the national economy.

However, as societies cannot be formed only with scientific developments, there is a need for gifted education also in the arts, music, languages and culture (S. S. Han, 2005). Thus, in the future, there not only needs to be a focus in gifted education in the sciences but also in other diverse areas. Gifted education policy must also be made to encourage a more proportionate and balanced education curriculum (Y. E. Kim, 2000).

b. Lack of Teacher Training

Another issue that arose from the data collected is the lack of trained teachers in the area of gifted and leadership education. It was reported that current teachers in gifted and leadership education lack expertise. For the success of gifted education, the professional expert teachers of gifted education are necessary (H. W. Kim, 2003, p. 112). However, the gifted education teachers teaching in institutes presently are those who have only qualified for mainstream schools. According to research in 2002, only 19.2% of the teachers who were teaching gifted students had received gifted education training (Cho, Kim, Park, and Chung, 2002). It was found that out of the 700 teachers who received gifted education training only 47 teachers went on to contribute as a gifted student teacher (S. H. Cho, 2005).

In this sense, training for educating gifted students should be given to a larger teacher population, and the teaching staff in every school should be given more opportunities to learn more about gifted education through workshops and training courses. In addition, administrative help should be given so that the teachers should be led to use their specialities to their full potential when teaching gifted children. Furthermore, self-research study of the teachers is equally effective. Financial support should be available for self-research, aiding teachers to study abroad to learn different teaching methods to gain the expertise of gifted education. Permanent professional gifted education teachers should be stationed in the gifted institutions for them to have proficiency in their teaching sector, rather than to employ several part-time staff who teach mainstream children (Yoon and Park, 2003).

c. Change in Gifted Stereotypes in Culture, Society and Parental Thoughts

The data results revealed that there are some misconceptions about gifted students in the Korean society due to traditional thoughts. The general misconception of Koreans is that special needs education is urgently important, whilst gifted education is seen as an optional luxury or "bourgeois education" (S. H. Cho, 2002a, p. 202). In addition, parents of the non-gifted students fear that their children might be disadvantaged in entering higher education.

These personal reasons partly lead to underdevelopment of gifted education. One of largest problems in Korean education currently is that children are forcedly given gifted education in private institutes since a young age to encourage 'typical' ability children into gifted children. Specialists point out that the private institutes have the children memorise gifted identification tests prior to taking the test. However, such preliminary learning under the title of gifted education does not help to develop giftedness and may lead children to feel inadequate or stressed. Kenny (cited from H. G. Lee, 2005) maintains that such private education may make children become familiar with entrance examinations and gifted programmes, but the children will experience difficulties especially with peers in the gifted schools and their achievements of learning are likely to fall below 'average.' Emphasising the need for entering into a gifted programme may cause problems in the healthy development of children. This type of gifted education conducted by private educations does not enhance the abilities of students but tends to destroy their creative abilities as they are made to memorise and practice gifted entrance examinations (H. G. Lee, 2005).

In order to prevent such harmful consequences, the aims and the processes involved in gifted education can be made aware by specialists in the field to a wider population. Gifted education institutes could invite specialists to inform the parents and students as well as help run gifted programmes. In order to inform the Korean people about the true concept of gifted education, specialists and researchers in gifted education should be consulted by the teachers to firmly establish gifted education as a national special education system rather than a means to acceleration and entering better universities.

d. No Appropriate Gifted Programme

The participant teachers also expressed the lack of comprehensive gifted programmes in Korea. It was believed that the current gifted education programmes in Korea are not suitable as they only focus on knowledge and learning of academic concepts. Although gifted students have project investigations, they are very much theoretical and do not focus on the process or methods of learning such as finding resources, understanding the material and finding results.

Thus, diverse gifted educational programmes should be developed, taking into account the needs of schools and their situations. Gifted education programmes must also be systematic so that students can be categorised into the different abilities that they have. Hence, a curriculum must be made focusing on various ages of the children, with funding and support from the government (Gallagher, 2002).

The gifted programmes should also include the non-academic subject areas and facilities outside the school should also be used to develop the current gifted programmes. For instance, research museums, music centres, art centres, and science centres can be utilised outside the school times during weekends or holidays. An example can be seen in the Australian Gifted Interest Centre.

In addition, gifted programmes must also include some ethical teaching as well for the mental and spiritual growth to equip them in becoming the future leaders in their fields. The significance of moral and character-building education was supported by Seok Hee Cho, the director of Korean Educational Development Institute, who stated that gifted children are only taught knowledge in school, but their personal and moral development is not considered in gifted schools. In this sense, moral education will be focused on in the suggestions for a model gifted programme.

How Far Are Good Leaders Born or Made?

The results showed that teachers thought that not all gifted students have leadership skills and therefore only a small minority of gifted students have leadership skills to be developed. Many traits of gifted pupils have been found to be the same as those with leadership abilities. The common traits of good leaders and gifted students include: language skills, sociability, vision towards the future, problem solving, critical thinking, challenging new things, responsibility, and self-satisfaction (Black, 1984; Karnes and Bean, 2001; Plowman, 1981). Furthermore, many leaders were found to have a high IQ of 115-130 (Hollingworth, 1926) or in other words, many gifted children acted as 'leaders' in school (Terman, 1925).

Although there is the perspective that leaders are 'born' and therefore, leadership is innate, many believe that one cannot become a leader with just leadership potential (Kim, 1998). However, there are views that specific leadership skills can be learned (Rodd, 1994, p. 6). Renzulli (1978) believed that the top 15-20% of all students have the potential to become international leaders provided they are educated in leadership, highlighting the significance of education. In contrast, those who hold the trait perspective suggest that certain individuals have special innate or inborn characteristics or make them leaders, and it is these qualities that differentiate them from non-leaders. Some of the personal qualities used to identify leaders include unique physical factors such as height, personality features such as extroversion, and ability characteristics such as speech fluency (Bryman, 1992). There are some inherited personal attributes which are associated with leadership.

There are various evidences to support the innate account. There are three main types of innate talent accounts (Howe, 1999; Howe et al., 1998). Firstly, there is much popular evidence that very young children have innate talents such as those who are able to talk early or to play instruments at an early age. However, there are limitations to evidences. For instance, the childhood descriptions of gifted children are usually made by parents in hindsight. Hence, these recollections may not always be accurate. These evidences put emphasis in the talents of the children and do not mention the possible opportunities that they had. An example is that of Amadeus Mozart who we all know to have possessed great innate musical skills. However, many researches fail to mention the opportunities that he was given through his musical father (Howe, 1997).

The second type of evidence for the innate accounts of giftedness is the existence of children who possess extraordinary musical skills such as having 'perfect pitch'. Yet, these accounts cannot be innate, although the children who have these skills are extremely young. They are nevertheless, a "learned capacity" (Howe, 1999, p. 163).

Thirdly, there are some evidences which underlines that those with extraordinary capabilities can be correlated to brain functioning. However, Howe (1999) points out that no selective brain activity is yet directly related to certain capabilities a person might have. Secondly, he emphasises that the "fact that two qualities are related is not really sufficient evidence for the existence of such a cause and effect association" (Howe, 1999, p. 163).

In addition, there has been some research in the observations of babies of different nationalities and finding possibly innate differences in them. For instance, differences in European and African babies were observed in Kenya by Super (1979) whereby he found that Kipsigi infants showed motor developments such as sitting and walking a month earlier than the counterpart European infants. However, Super (1979) found that there were other motor skills which the Kipsigi babies were slower at developing, such as crawling or lifting of the head. It was then when it was found that the Kipsigi mothers had taught their children to walk and sit constantly as they even had specialised words of instruction for sitting and walking (Howe, 1999, p. 14).

On the other hand, Galton (1822-1911) who contributed much development in the research of intelligence and intelligence testing understood intelligence as being hereditary. He was very much influenced by the evolutionary theories of Darwin. His book called, 'Hereditary Genius' stated that high intelligence is genetic. Modern day psychologists such as Gage and Berliner (1988) followed Galton's ideas of intelligence and reported that 75-80% of intelligence is hereditary whilst only 20% of intelligence is influenced by the environment. However, the majority of psychologists or educators now believe that the environment plays a large factor in the development of intelligence or giftedness (Chung, Im, and Chung, 2004).

In conclusion, on the issue of whether giftedness in any area is innate or is a talent, Howe (1999) simply comments, "the fact that a trait is partly inherited does not usually rule out the possibility of it being radically modified by environmental influences" (pp. 101-102). In other words, in terms of leadership skills, there are innate and inherited skills, with leadership skills being one of them. However, there are also strong educational factors which contribute towards leadership development (Kim and Choi, 2005).

Curricula and Teaching Materials

In the development of particular skills, various programmes or curricula used is very important: "Gifted skills are generally improved and progressed through education with programmes or curricula" (Karnes et al., 2001, p. 227). However, the interviews confirmed the belief that Korea is in need of leadership development programmes or curricula.

One interviewee teacher who led gifted programmes said that 90% of the currently used teaching materials in leadership development were activities of other subjects. These materials were said to be theoretical and impractical. The materials were not systematic either, and therefore it could be seen that a more practical curriculum and materials are in need. For instance, in Central Elementary School in Indiana, United States, diverse and special activities were made for leadership education. Every special class had a different research topic chosen every year which lead them the class to plan and research about it, often in relation to their local communities. Through practical project work such as these, the children were able to participate and learned a lot about partnerships. The teachers were able to develop teamwork, effort, problem solving, modelling, and social skills (I. S. Lee, 1995).

In summary, according to the interviews, the currently used leadership curricula are too theory based and wanted a more practical and realistic curriculum. Secondly, they believed that the current leadership curricula do not involve moral education and do not develop social and emotional aspects. Thirdly, it was found that there are not many trained teachers in gifted and leadership education. Hence, detailed teacher instructions or guidelines should also be written so that they are informed specifically how they can lead their lessons. It was found that more directions, strategies or guidelines for teachers of gifted children would also be useful.

Leadership Education and Moral Education

The Korean culture considers moral education as significant as social etiquette and ethics are emphasised due to the cultural background in Confucianism (Wong and Evers, 2001, p. 37). In Eastern cultures, moral education is a valued part of leadership education as Wong (2001) discusses the relationship in the Chinese context: "[China] has a long history of valuing leadership and preparing leaders on moral grounds" (p. 37). May (1971) also supports this view as he says, "The child's education would be incomplete without moral education. Therefore some direct moral teaching is essential in the classroom as well as at home" (p. 164). He continued to add, "Some moral education lessons might be devoted to the study of famous people, especially reformers and missionaries. Suitable material could easily be obtained, many teachers believed from varied biographical sources" (May, 1971, p. 77).

It was found that gifted leaders 'combine high intelligence with deep feelings of emotional connectedness with others' (Dabrowski, 1972; Piechowski, 1986, 1991). In addition, gifted students tend to be sensitive to any moral conflicts in everyday life. Gifted children do not need to be taught how they can behave morally in various situations, but it could prove more effective to provide opportunities for them to search and think for themselves regarding various moral problems that they may face. There needs to be more thoughts and discussions on self-experience and understanding of morality, experience of thinking of being in another person's shoes, helping others in difficult situations, judging the appropriate behaviour in various situations, the difference between social and anti-social behaviours. Sometimes, it may prove to be a valuable method of learning for the children to see a person modelling behaviour from someone who has a high level of moral reasoning (Chung et al., 2004).

Amongst many opinions expressed in the interviews, teachers said that the schools must give moral training because they thought so many parents did not. However, the moral education taught at schools was not enough and one suggested the development of more pragmatic ethical education.

However, May (1971) believed that moral training is related to personal human development and therefore must be taught at home as there is not enough time to teach it in classrooms and most teachers would agree that ideally, moral training is best given in the home (May, 1971). In the interviews, a teacher also believed that moral education was the task of the home, not the school whereas one believed it was the church's responsibility. Conclusively, moral education should occur both at the home and also in school. In particular, moral education should be given through everyday living whether it be in the family, school or at church.

Feldhusen and Kennedy (1988) stated that leadership talent involves intellectual ability, moral development, thinking skills, social/personal behaviours and the ability increase others' motivation. As education is emphasised in human development in Korean culture, the emphasis of education is put in nurturing the children into adults. Hence, ethics and moral education is a crucial aspect of their personal development (K. W. Jun, 2000). In addition, Koreans believe that leadership is heavily associated with morality and social relationships (Kim, 1998). Thus, in Korean culture, moral education is an integral part of leadership education.

Conclusion

Overall, the results showed that there is a lack of leadership gifted education in Korea despite the demand for a systematic, coherent and independent leadership gifted curricula. The teachers also expressed a clear vision of what should constitute such education. These results depict the fertile soil of the current situation of Korean gifted education in which the prospective leadership gifted curriculum/programme could take root and flourish.

REFERENCES

Black, J. D. (1984). *Leadership: A new model particularly applicable to gifted youth*. Indiana, PA: ERIC Clearinghouse on Handicapped and Gifted Children. (ERIC Document Reproduction Service No. ED253990)

Bryman, A. (1992). *Charisma and leadership in organizations*. London: Sage.

Cawood, J. (1984). *The modern school's role in socialising the gifted student leader*. Unpublished doctoral dissertation, University of Stellenbosch, South Africa.

Cho, S. H. (2000, April). *Current state of art in Korean education for the gifted in math and research*. Presented at the 18th annual conference of the Mathematical Education Symposium. Seoul National University, Korea (in Korean).

Cho, S. H. (2002a). Identification and screening of the gifted. Busan In Board of Education (Ed.). *Theory and practice of gifted education*. Series of Busan Education. Busan: Busan Research Center for Educational Science (in Korean).

Cho, S. H. (2005). Korean educational strategies for the gifted and talented. *Symposium for Advanced Education and Gifted Education Policies* (pp. 23-52). Seoul: Korean Educational Development Institute Press (in Korean).

Cho, S. H., Kim, H. W., Park, S. I., and Chung, H. C. (2002). *Comprehensive Plan for Gifted Education Promotion (CR2002-56)*. Seoul: Korean Education Development Institute Press (in Korean).

Chung, S., Im, H. S., and Chung, C. K. (2004). *An introduction into children's gifted education*. Seoul: Chung Song (in Korean).

Cohen, L., Manion, L., and Morrison, K. (2000). *Research Methods in Education* (5th ed.). New York: RoutledgeFalmer.

Dabrowski, K. (1972). *Psychoneurosis is not an illness*. London: Gryf.

Feldhusen, J. F., and Kennedy, D. M. (1988). Observing the Nature and Emergence of Leadership Talent Among Gifted Youth. *Gifted Child Today (GCT), 11*(6), 2-7.

Gage, N. L., and Berliner, D. C. (1988). *Educational psychology*. Boston, MA: Houghton Mifflin.

Gallagher, J. J. (2002). *Society's role in educating gifted students: The role of public policy*. Senior Scholars Series. Storrs, CT: National Research Center on the Gifted and Talented, University of Connecticut. (ERIC Document Reproduction Service No. ED476370)

Gallagher, J. J., Weiss, P., Oglesby, K., and Thomas, T. (1983). *The status of gifted/talented education: United States surveys of needs, practices, and policies*. Ventura County, CA: Ventura County Superintendent of Schools Office.

Glaser, B. G. and Strauss, A. L. (1967). *The Discovery of Grounded Theory: Strategies for Qualitative Research*. Chicago: Aldine Publishing Company.

Han, S. S. (2005). *A basic study of the psychological characteristics and development of language-creative gifted students.* Seoul: Korean Educational Development Institute Press (in Korean).

Hollingworth, L. S. (1926). *Gifted children: Their nature and nurture.* New York: Macmillan.

Howe, M. J. A. (1997). *IQ in question: The truth about intelligence.* London: Sage.

Howe, M. J. A. (1999). *The psychology of high abilities.* London: Macmillan.

Howe, M. J. A., Davidson, J. W., and Sloboda, J. A. (1998). Innate Talents: Reality or Myth? *Behavioral and Brain Sciences, 21*(3), 399-442.

Jun, K. W. (2000). *Korean gifted/talented/creative education for the new millennium.* Seoul: Hak Moon Sa.

Karnes F. A. and Bean S. M. (Eds.). (2001). *Methods and materials for teaching the gifted and talented.* Waco, TX: Prufrock Press.

Kim, H. W. (2003). *Direction of the development of gifted education.* Je Ju Do: Je Ju Do Education Department (in Korean).

Kim, J. H. (1998). *Manual of Judgment of Gifted Students.* Seoul: Wonmisa (in Korean).

Kim, M. S. (2004). Pastoral Leadership as a Servant: Servant Leadership and its Effect on Management Church Organization. *The Journal of Business Administration Management Research Centre College of Business Administration Ewha Woman's University, 4*(1), page unknown.

Kim, O. H. and Choi, I. S. (2005). *Teacher Leadership.* Gyonggi Province: Korean Academic Information (in Korean).

Kim, Y. E. (2000). *The effect of self-development programmes on human relationships and self-esteem.* Unpublished master's thesis, Kun Kook University, South Korea (in Korean).

Lee, H. G. (2005). *Understanding of Gifted Education Policy.* Seoul: Ministry of Education and Human Resources (in Korean).

Lee, I. S., (September, 1995). Special Activities of the Art Classes in American Central Elementary School which Cultivates Artistic Talent and Leadership. *Our Education Journal*, pp. 182-186 (in Korean)

Marland, S. P. (1972). *Education of the gifted and talented: Report to the congress of the United States by the U.S. Commissioner of Education.* Washington, DC: U.S. Government Printing Office.

May, P. R. (1971). *Moral education in school.* London: Methuen Educational.

Piechowski, M. M. (1986). The Concept of Developmental Potential. *Roeper Review, 8*(3), 190-197.

Piechowski, M. M. (1991). Emotional development and emotional giftedness. In N. Colangelo and G. A. Davis (Eds.), *A handbook of gifted education* (pp. 285-306). Needham Heights, MA: Allyn and Bacon.

Plowman, P. D. (1981). Training Extraordinary Leaders. *Roeper Review, 3*(3), 13-16.

Renzulli, J. S. (1978). What Makes Giftedness? Re-examining a Definition. *Phi Delta Kappan, 60*(3), 180-184.

Rodd, J. (1994). *Leadership in early childhood: The pathway to professionalism.* Buckingham: Open University Press.

Silverman, L. K. (1993). Social development, leadership and gender issues. In L. K. Silverman (Ed.) *Counseling the Gifted and Talented.* (pp. 291-327) Denver, CO: Love.

Suh, H. E., Son, Y. A., and Kim, G. J. (2003). *Current status of teaching and learning at educational institutions for the gifted.* Seoul: Korean Educational Development Institute Press (in Korean).

Super, C. (1976). Environmental Effects on Motor Development: The Case of 'African Infant Precocity.' *Developmental Medicine and Child Neurology, 18*(5), 561-7.

Terman, L. M. (1925). *Genetic studies of genius* (Vols. 1-5). Stanford, CA: Stanford University Press.

Verma, G. K., and Mallick, K. (1999). *Researching education: Perspectives and techniques.* London: Falmer Press.

Wong, K. C. (2001). Culture and educational leadership. In K. C. Wong and C. W. Evers (Eds.). *Leadership for quality schooling: International perspectives* (pp. 36-53). London: Routledge Falmer.

Yoon, J. I., and Park, S. I. (2003). *Consolidation of educational system for the gifted in science.* Seoul: Korean Education Development Institute Press (in Korean).

INDEX

A

abuse, vii, 21, 48
academic performance, 87, 92
access, 98
accessibility, 43
accountability, 59, 60, 66, 69
adaptation, 44
adaptations, 100
administrators, 99
adolescents, vii, 21, 40, 42, 45, 47, 49, 51
adulthood, 49
adults, 87, 90, 126
advancement, 91
Africa, 127
age, 32, 72, 112, 114, 121, 123
agencies, 25
aggression, vii, 21, 23, 24, 28, 29, 32, 34, 35, 37, 39, 40, 41, 52
aggression scales, 29
AIDS, 50
alcohol abuse, vii, 21
alcohol use, viii, 21, 23, 24, 28, 29, 32, 33, 37, 39, 51
American Psychological Association, 42, 48
analytical framework, 16
ANOVA, 32, 34, 35, 36
anxiety, 47, 105
appointments, 60, 62, 65, 68
appraisals, 38
aptitude, 111
Argentina, 60
Asia, 56
assessment, 64, 65, 69, 74, 89, 105
assets, 89
asymmetry, 46
atmosphere, 99, 105
attachment, 50
attitude measurement, 34
attitudes, viii, 21, 22, 24, 28, 32, 33, 37, 40, 96, 104, 105, 106, 107
authority, 59, 60, 62, 65, 67, 68, 69, 77, 93
autonomy, 67
awareness, viii, 66, 71, 91, 113

B

base, vii, 9, 59, 63, 64, 68, 70, 91, 109
basic education, 74
beginning teachers, 109
benchmarks, 62
benefits, viii, 22, 31, 40, 41, 47, 51, 57, 75, 88, 89, 91
BI, 29
bias, viii, 21, 24, 28, 30, 32, 35, 36, 37, 39, 40, 42, 46, 114
blame, 90
blueprint, 62
body of evidence, vii, 21
body size, 48

brain activity, 123
brain functioning, 123
bullying, 51
bureaucracy, 60

C

caregivers, viii, 71, 73, 74, 76, 79, 81, 83, 84, 85, 91, 92
case studies, 18
case study, vii, 1
certification, 99, 109
challenges, 2, 25, 60, 70
Chicago, 128
childhood, 45, 48, 50, 123, 129
childrearing, 87
child-rearing practices, 87
children, viii, 45, 47, 48, 52, 71, 72, 73, 74, 75, 76, 77, 78, 79, 81, 82, 83, 84, 85, 86, 87, 88, 89, 90, 91, 92, 93, 94, 101, 112, 116, 117, 120, 121, 122, 123, 124, 125, 126, 127, 128
China, vii, 77, 84, 92, 94, 125
Christians, 46
chronic diseases, 50
citizens, 87
clarity, 42
classes, 7, 90, 115, 116
classification, 76
classroom, 2, 3, 4, 5, 6, 7, 8, 10, 11, 14, 15, 16, 18, 97, 98, 101, 104, 107, 125
classroom management, 97
classroom settings, 8
classroom teacher, 98
cleaning, 25, 26
clinical psychology, 48
clothing, 25
coding, 119
cognitive level, 15, 19
coherence, 66
collaboration, 8, 98, 106
college students, 42, 44, 48
Colombia, 60
communication, 8, 76, 99, 108
communication skills, 76
communication technologies, 99
communities, 4, 84, 98, 106, 124
community, 8, 50, 91, 99, 105, 107
competition, 38
compilation, 114
comprehension, 75, 76, 85, 86
Comprehensive Social Security Assistance, 74
computer, 79
conception, 6, 15, 17
conditioning, 43
conference, 127
confidentiality, 114
conflict, 46
Confucianism, 88, 90, 92, 125
congress, 129
consent, 114
construct validity, 49
construction, 42
consulting, 100, 105
contour, 108
control group, 25, 33
conversations, 10, 88
cooking, 25
cooperation, 25, 26, 27, 39, 61
cost, 39, 41, 52, 60, 77
Council of Ministers, 2, 17
creative abilities, 121
critical thinking, 122
criticism, 32
CT, 40, 127
cultural norms, 92
culture, viii, 71, 84, 87, 88, 89, 90, 92, 112, 117, 120, 125, 126
curricula, vii, 1, 2, 112, 124, 125, 126
curriculum, 2, 6, 7, 9, 16, 17, 18, 58, 62, 63, 64, 65, 68, 69, 72, 97, 100, 109, 120, 122, 124, 125, 126

D

danger, 62
data analysis, 102
data collection, 6, 113
decentralisation, 60

Index

decentralization, 70
deficit, 60
Delta, 109, 129
depression, 47
depressive symptoms, 44, 50
depth, 63, 68, 78, 81, 112, 113, 114
developed countries, 58
developed nations, 59
developing countries, 58
deviation, 80, 82
dimensionality, 50
dinosaurs, 76
directionality, 45
disclosure, 114
discrimination, 40, 46, 47
diseases, 50
distance education, 99, 100
distance learning, 96
distribution, 30, 102
diversity, 68
drawing, 4
drugs, 23, 29, 33, 34, 35, 54, 55

E

echoing, 16
economic downturn, 60
economic status, 71, 86, 90
editors, iv
education, vii, 17, 18, 19, 46, 59, 60, 61, 64, 69, 70, 72, 74, 83, 84, 85, 86, 87, 88, 89, 90, 91, 94, 96, 99, 100, 105, 107, 108, 110, 112, 113, 115, 116, 117, 118, 119, 120, 121, 122, 124, 125, 126, 127, 128, 129
education reform, 60, 61, 105, 107
educational experience, vii, 21
educational institutions, 129
educational services, 59
educational system, 58, 112, 129
educators, 97, 99, 105, 106, 110, 124
electricity, 97
elementary level science teachers, viii, 95, 107
elementary school, 88, 99, 106, 117

elementary students, 4
elementary teachers, 3, 17, 104, 107
e-mail, 10
emergency, 27
empirical studies, 58
employment, 99
empowerment, 70, 85, 88
encouragement, 25
environment, viii, 31, 63, 64, 69, 71, 72, 73, 76, 77, 78, 79, 80, 81, 82, 89, 91, 94, 106, 124
environmental factors, 89
environmental influences, 124
equality, 25
equipment, 25
ESR, 62
ethics, 116, 125, 126
ethnicity, 52, 114
etiquette, 125
euphoria, 31
evaluative conditioning, 43
everyday life, 125
evidence, vii, viii, 3, 21, 57, 58, 59, 68, 73, 112, 123
exaggeration, 75
examinations, 86, 90, 121
exercise, 27
expert teacher, 98, 120
expertise, 48, 120
exposure, 38, 106
external influences, 38

F

facilitators, 5, 8
factor analysis, 49
families, viii, 71, 72, 73, 74, 75, 77, 78, 79, 82, 83, 84, 87, 88, 89
family environment, 91
family income, 74
family members, 81
fear, 121
federally funded research initiative, viii, 95
feelings, 31, 125
fights, 55

financial, 42
fish, 49
fitness, 49
flexibility, 59, 60, 62, 67
focus groups, 106
force, 104
foster youth, 25
foundations, 19, 44
freedom, 59, 77, 79, 81
frequency distribution, 102
funding, 62, 122
funds, 30

G

gifted, 111, 112, 113, 115, 116, 117, 118, 119, 120, 121, 122, 123, 124, 125, 126, 127, 128, 129
giftedness, ix, 111, 112, 116, 118, 121, 123, 124, 129
globalization, 92
governance, 61, 63
government expenditure, 60
grades, 91, 96
grading, 59, 65, 68
group activities, 27
growth, 19, 51, 99, 109, 122
growth models, 51
guidance, 7, 105
guidelines, 125

H

happiness, 41
health, 41, 44, 50, 52
height, 27, 123
heightened self-esteem, vii, 21
high school, 49, 118
higher education, 99, 121
history, 18, 30, 88, 90, 97, 125
homes, 28
homework, 74, 75, 90
Hong Kong, vii, viii, 1, 2, 42, 57, 59, 60, 61, 62, 65, 68, 69, 70, 71, 72, 73, 74, 75, 77, 78, 82, 84, 86, 88, 89, 90, 91, 92, 93, 94

host, 2, 40
hostility, 51
housing, 74, 77, 93
human, 89, 116, 126, 128
human development, 126
Hunter, 21, 22, 23, 25, 37, 39, 44, 46
hypothesis, 11, 24, 36, 37, 51

I

ideal, 48
ideals, 90
identification, 46, 121
identity, 25, 41, 45, 46, 47, 48, 51
image, 51
immersion, 67
immigrants, 40
improvements, 23, 24, 31, 36, 58
income, 74, 84, 88, 93
individuals, 23, 24, 30, 36, 38, 39, 47, 122
Indonesia, 86
industry, 87, 89
infants, 123
infrastructure, 96
ingroup bias, 42
institutions, 61, 88, 99, 119, 120, 129
instructional materials, 6
instructional practice, 4
integration, 48
intelligence, 124, 125, 128
interaction effects, 32, 35, 36
interdependence, 25, 90
internal consistency, 102
interpersonal relations, 90
intervention, vii, 21, 23, 24, 28, 29, 30, 31, 32, 33, 35, 36, 37, 38, 39, 40
intimidation, 105
investment, 89, 119
issues, 28, 42, 52, 70, 100, 114, 129

J

Japan, 93
Jordan, 23, 37, 39, 47
junior high school, 118

K

Kenya, 123
kindergarten, 75, 84
Korea, vii, 111, 113, 115, 116, 117, 118, 119, 121, 124, 126, 127, 128

L

lack of opportunities, 106
landscape, 92
language proficiency, 75, 77, 87, 92
language skills, 72, 122
languages, 86, 120
lead, viii, 22, 26, 37, 41, 72, 96, 101, 114, 115, 121, 124, 125
leadership, ix, 27, 62, 63, 65, 96, 100, 101, 105, 107, 111, 112, 113, 114, 115, 116, 117, 118, 120, 122, 124, 125, 126, 127, 129
leadership abilities, 122
leadership characteristics, 116
leadership development, 113, 115, 124
leadership style, 63, 65
learners, 3
learning, vii, viii, 1, 2, 5, 6, 7, 8, 9, 10, 11, 13, 14, 15, 16, 17, 18, 19, 25, 45, 46, 57, 58, 59, 61, 63, 64, 66, 68, 69, 70, 71, 72, 77, 84, 85, 87, 88, 89, 91, 92, 94, 96, 97, 98, 99, 100, 105, 107, 108, 109, 117, 121, 126, 129
learning environment, 63, 64, 69
learning outcomes, viii, 57, 58, 59, 63, 66, 68, 70
learning process, 89
leisure, 74, 79, 90
lesson plan, 9, 11, 13
librarians, 88
light, vii, 34, 104
Likert scale, viii, 29, 95, 103
literacy, vii, 1, 2, 17, 75, 77, 85, 86, 88, 91, 92, 93, 94
living environment, 77
longitudinal study, 92
love, 41, 86, 92

M

magazines, 76
magnetism, 97
Mainland China, 77, 84
majority, 75, 124
management, vii, viii, 13, 14, 52, 57, 58, 61, 62, 66, 67, 69, 70, 97
manipulation, 32, 39
marriage, 107
Marx, 50
mass, 82, 87
mass media, 82, 87
materials, 6, 7, 9, 11, 13, 15, 17, 18, 76, 77, 78, 79, 80, 81, 82, 83, 85, 90, 98, 105, 107, 109, 124, 128
mathematics, 17, 19, 28, 53, 115, 119
matter, 97
measurement, 28, 32, 34, 35, 36, 42, 50
media, 19, 82, 87
median, 102
mentor, 96, 106
mentoring, viii, 95, 100, 104, 106, 107, 115
messages, 76
meta-analysis, 40, 72
Ministry of Education, 128
Minneapolis, 18
misconceptions, 120
mission, 118
modelling, 45, 80, 81, 82, 89, 90, 91, 124, 126
models, 4, 6, 44, 51, 81, 84, 89, 92, 100
Montana, 99
Moon, 128
moral development, 122, 126
moral reasoning, 126
moral training, 126
morality, 116, 125, 126
motivation, 25, 45, 86, 126
motor skills, 123
multidimensional, 49
museums, 122
music, 119, 120, 122

Index

N

naming, 52
narcissism, 40, 41, 48
National Research Council, 2, 19
nature of science (NOS), vii, 1, 2
negative attitudes, 32
negative consequences, 24, 37, 39
negative effects, 24
negative outcome behaviours, vii, 21
negative outcomes, viii, 22, 32, 37, 39, 40, 46
negativity, 107
neglect, 92
negotiation, 61
neutral, 101
New Zealand, vii, 21, 24, 25, 30, 50, 52
newspaper coverage, 63
Nicaragua, 60
NRC, 2, 19
nursing, 50
nurturance, 90

O

opportunities, 4, 5, 7, 8, 14, 16, 25, 26, 76, 85, 99, 106, 120, 123, 125
originality, 58
osmosis, 90

P

parental involvement, 72, 85, 86, 87, 91, 92, 93
parental support, 73, 84
parenting, 87
parents, viii, 28, 53, 56, 71, 72, 73, 74, 75, 76, 77, 78, 79, 81, 82, 83, 84, 85, 86, 87, 88, 89, 90, 91, 92, 115, 120, 121, 123, 126
participants, vii, viii, 3, 5, 18, 21, 22, 23, 24, 25, 26, 27, 28, 30, 31, 32, 33, 37, 38, 39, 73, 95, 100, 101, 102, 104, 105, 106, 113, 114

pedagogical content knowledge (PCK), ix, 3, 9, 95, 96, 97, 104, 107
pedagogy, 4, 99, 108
peer group, 108
peer support, 84
personal computers, 25
personal development, 4, 126
personal learning, 85
personal qualities, 123
personality, 82, 90, 123
PGE, 31
Philadelphia, 108
physical abuse, 48
physical aggression, 29, 35
physical fitness, 49
physics, 2, 19, 97
pilot study, 44, 58
PISA, 73
pitch, 123
playing, 79
pleasure, 87
policy, 60, 62, 64, 65, 67, 69, 70, 120, 127
poor readers, 72
population, 98, 99, 120, 121
positive attitudes, 64, 69
positive feedback, 38
positive reinforcement, 27
positive relationship, 39
pregnancy, 52
prejudice, vii, 21, 23, 30, 40, 43, 44, 47
preparation, iv
preservice teachers, 98
primary school, 48, 72, 73, 91, 115
private education, 121
problem solving, 105, 118, 122, 124
professional development, vii, viii, 1, 2, 4, 5, 7, 8, 19, 60, 62, 65, 69, 95, 96, 98, 100, 101, 102, 104, 105, 106, 107, 108, 109
professional development (PD), viii, 95
professional growth, 99
professionalism, 59, 129
professionals, 47, 60, 98, 109
project, 4, 5, 6, 46, 68, 96, 100, 101, 102, 104, 105, 106, 107, 121, 124

prosperity, 88
protection, 42
prototype, 61, 111
psychology, 48, 52, 83, 127, 128
psychomotor ability, 111
psychosocial functioning, 40
public housing, 74, 77
public policy, 127
public schools, 61
public sector, 60
Pyszczynski, 22, 24, 37, 39, 40, 51

Q

questioning, 3, 76
questionnaire, 29, 31, 41, 42, 44, 49, 63, 64, 65, 67, 68, 73, 81

R

racism, 52
reactions, 43
reading, viii, 71, 72, 73, 74, 75, 76, 77, 78, 79, 80, 81, 82, 83, 84, 85, 86, 87, 88, 89, 90, 91, 92, 93
reading comprehension, 86
reading difficulties, 80, 81
reality, 112
reasoning, 6, 15, 126
recognition, 66, 68, 69
recommendations, 104
recreation, 47
recycling, 79
reform, vii, 1, 2, 8, 17, 19, 59, 62, 68, 72, 105, 107, 109
Reform, 17, 109, 110
reformers, 125
reforms, 60, 62, 70
regulations, 76
reinforcement, 27, 51
rejection, 50
relatives, 78, 84, 86
reliability, 29, 30, 50, 102, 113, 114
religious beliefs, 28, 53
research institutions, 99

researchers, 6, 22, 23, 72, 89, 113, 118, 121
resistance, 46
resources, 9, 16, 44, 46, 50, 59, 60, 73, 77, 78, 79, 84, 85, 91, 93, 98, 121
response, viii, 12, 14, 27, 71, 102
restaurants, 86, 90
restructuring, 61, 63
rights, 55
risk, 44, 52
root, 126
rules, 79
rural areas, 99
rural schools, viii, 95, 98, 105

S

safety, 27
school, vii, viii, 25, 28, 43, 48, 49, 53, 57, 58, 59, 60, 61, 62, 63, 64, 65, 67, 68, 69, 70, 72, 73, 75, 78, 82, 84, 85, 86, 87, 88, 89, 91, 94, 95, 96, 98, 102, 105, 106, 108, 109, 112, 113, 115, 116, 117, 120, 121, 122, 126, 127, 129
school performance, 72
school support, 85, 91
School-based Management (SBM), viii, 57
schooling, vii, 71, 84, 88, 89, 92, 93, 129
science, vii, viii, 1, 2, 3, 4, 6, 8, 15, 17, 18, 19, 95, 96, 97, 98, 99, 100, 101, 102, 104, 105, 106, 107, 108, 109, 110, 119, 122, 129
scientific knowledge, 3, 6
scientific method, 98
scope, 106
secondary school students, viii, 25, 57
secondary schools, 57, 61, 62, 68
self-concept, 41, 42, 43, 44, 47, 48, 49, 50, 52
self-confidence, 79
self-efficacy, 25, 26, 39, 42, 46, 82, 91
self-esteem, vii, 21, 22, 23, 24, 26, 28, 30, 31, 32, 33, 36, 37, 38, 39, 40, 41, 42, 43, 44, 45, 46, 47, 48, 50, 51, 52, 53, 128
self-evaluations, 45
self-image, 51

self-knowledge, 41
self-regard, 45
self-report data, 104
self-study, 91
self-view, 43
self-worth, 42, 43, 44, 45, 48
seminars, 83, 85
semi-structured interviews, 113
services, 59
sex, 25, 27, 28, 32, 49, 53
shape, 90
shortage, 99
showing, 8, 11, 38
siblings, 78, 83
skill acquisition, 91
sociability, 122
social behavior, 52
social behaviour, 125
society, viii, 50, 52, 60, 71, 73, 87, 88, 112, 117, 118, 120
socioeconomic status, 77, 89
sociology, 50
sociometer theory, 48
solution, 99
South Africa, 127
South Korea, 112, 113, 115, 128
Spain, 60
special education, 121
specialists, 121
specific knowledge, 83
speech, 123
spending, 87
stability, 50
stakeholders, 61, 62
standard deviation, 82
state, 39, 127
states, 74, 89, 99, 111
statistics, 74, 77, 93, 102
stock, 78
storytelling, 75, 76, 77, 83
stress, 44, 46, 51
stressors, 44
structure, 44, 49, 50, 63, 99, 113
student achievement, 72, 73
student teacher, 120

style, 63, 65, 104
subsidy, 60
substance use, 44
Sui dynasty, 89
supervision, 75
support staff, 100, 105
Sweden, 40
symptoms, 44, 50
synthesis, 46
systemic change, 96

T

talent, 123, 124, 126
Tang dynasty, 83
target, 35, 36
teacher attitudes, vii, ix, 95, 100, 101, 104, 106, 107, 108
teacher instruction, 125
teachers, vii, viii, 1, 2, 3, 4, 5, 6, 7, 8, 9, 10, 11, 12, 15, 16, 17, 18, 19, 59, 60, 62, 63, 65, 67, 68, 69, 88, 95, 96, 97, 98, 100, 101, 102, 104, 105, 106, 107, 108, 109, 112, 113, 115, 116, 117, 120, 121, 122, 124, 125, 126
teaching experience, 16, 113
teaching strategies, 99, 118
team members, 100, 105
teams, 5, 98, 100, 105, 107
techniques, viii, 3, 71, 82, 83, 85, 91, 97, 129
technology, 17, 106, 107, 119
telephone, 10, 114
telephone conversations, 10
testing, 42, 124
test-retest reliability, 29, 30
textbook, 74
Thailand, 61
therapeutic community, 50
therapy, 47
thermodynamics, 97
thoughts, 120, 125
threats, 23, 46, 114
time constraints, 28
time series, 44

trainees, 23, 24, 25, 27, 28, 33, 38, 48
training, 9, 24, 25, 33, 36, 37, 39, 46, 49, 50, 60, 83, 84, 106, 115, 120, 126
training programs, 49
traits, 98, 122
translation, 88
transparency, 59, 66
treatment, 44
trial, 5, 6, 7, 8, 9, 13, 16
triangulation, 10, 68
tuition, 87
turnover, 99

U

UK, 19, 30, 52
uniform, 62
United Kingdom, 56
United States, viii, 5, 93, 95, 124, 128, 129
universities, 61, 121
urban, 98

V

validation, 51
variables, 28, 32, 34, 35
vein, 72, 91
Venezuela, 60
verbal aggression, viii, 21, 23, 24, 28, 29, 32, 34, 35, 37, 39
victims, 48

videos, 6, 7, 9, 10, 14, 15, 16
videotape, 108
violence, 40, 41, 55
vision, 122, 126
vocabulary, 29, 53, 76
voyage programme lead, viii, 22
vulnerability, 52
Vygotsky, 98

W

walking, 123
Washington, 19, 42, 48, 99, 110, 129
watches, 27
weakness, 39
wealth, 89
web, 27, 108
websites, 63
Western countries, 59, 61, 62
wilderness, 47, 51
workplace, 109
World Wide Web, 73, 74
worldwide, 58
worry, 29, 53

Y

Yale University, 44
young people, 46
youth development voyage, vii, 21, 30